HANET - CANTERE

C000178248

RNE BAY · SANDWICH · WHITSTAB

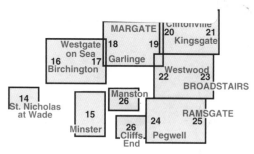

MARGATE
Cliftonville 20   21
Westgate on Sea 18   19   Kingsgate
16   17
Birchington   Garlinge
Westwood 22   23
BROADSTAIRS

14
St. Nicholas at Wade

Manston 26
15
Minster
26
Cliffs. Pegwell
End
24   25
RAMSGATE

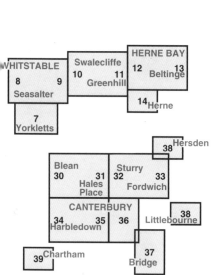

WHITSTABLE
8   9
Seasalter
Swalecliffe 10   11
Greenhill
HERNE BAY 12   13
Beltinge
14 Herne

7
Yorkletts

38 Hersden

Blean 30   31
Hales Place
Sturry 32   33
Fordwich

CANTERBURY
34   35   36
Harbledown
Littlebourne 38

39 Chartham
37 Bridge

Ash 27
SANDWICH
28   29
Woodnesborough
27 Eastry

Every effort has been made to verify the accuracy of information in this book but the publishers cannot accept responsibility for expense or loss caused by an error or omission. Information that will be of assistance to the user of the maps will be welcomed.

The representation on these maps of a road, track or path is no evidence of the existence of a right of way.

Car Park   P

Public Convenience   C

Place of Worship   +

One-way Street   →

Pedestrianized

Post Office   ●

Scale of street plans 4 inches to 1 mile
Unless otherwise stated

eet plans prepared and published by ESTATE PUBLICATIONS, Bridewell House, TENTERDEN, KENT. The Publishers acknowledge the co-operation of the local authorities of towns represented in this atlas.

Ordnance Survey® This product includes mapping data licensed from Ordnance Survey® with the permission of the Controller of Her Majesty's Stationery Office.

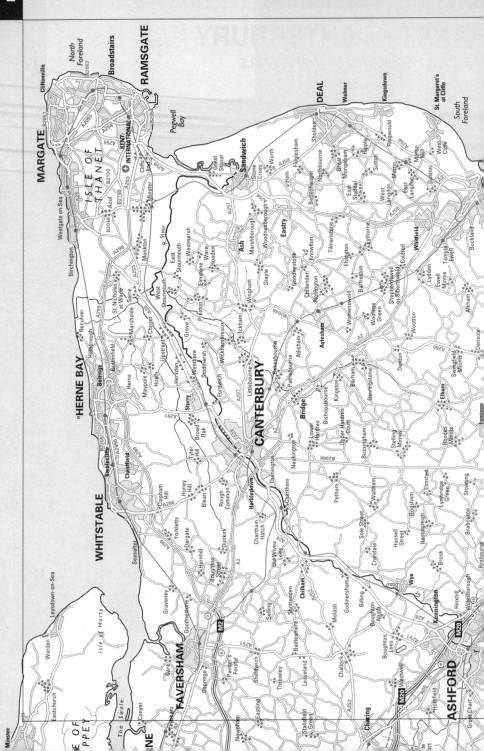

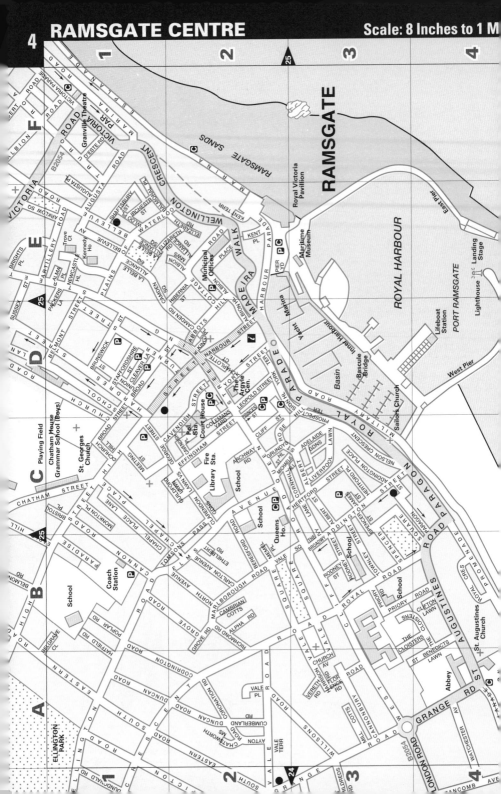

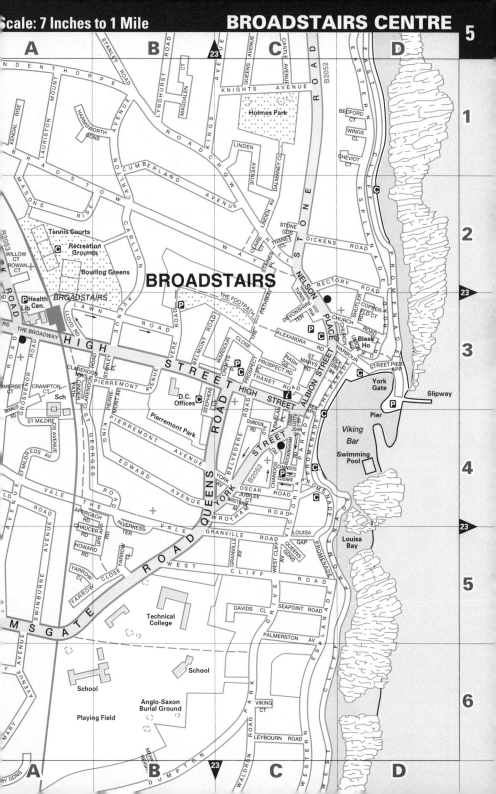

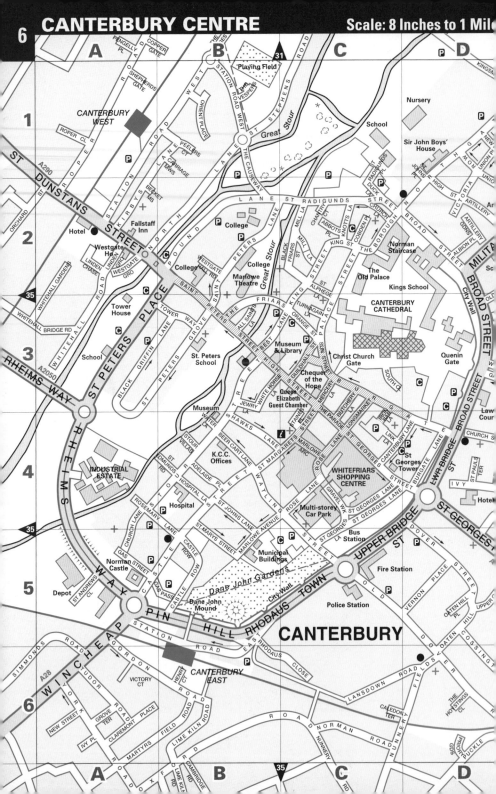

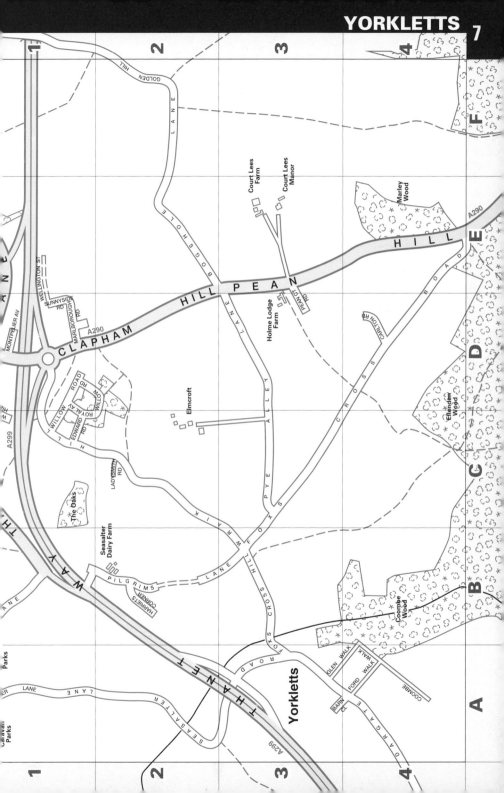

Yorkletts

A   B   C   D

1

2

COAST
ALLE

WA
CRI

3

WEST BEACH

SAXON
SHORE

Golf

THE   O A Z E

Seasalter

SEASALTER BEACH

JOY
LANE
METEOR
VALKYRIE
AVENUE

COLUMBIA
GENESTA
SUNRAY
CUNDISHALL
CL

Joy Lane
Schools

PARADE FAIRWAY ADMIRALTY
CRES
WK
SHAMROCK
BRITANNIA
CYPRESS
CL

GROVE
JOY
ROAD
FLORENCE AVENUE
GEORGES
MEDINA AV
ALPHEGE
ST
SOMERSET
CL
APRIL
RISE
NORVIEW RD
AVENUE
SHEARWATER
CL
KING
5

PRESTON
HAZLEMERE
CORYLUS
DR
SHAMROCK
AV
SCEPTRE
WY
HAWK
OSPREY CL
RD

Blue
Anchor
(P.H.)
ALLAN ROAD
HODGSON
RD
BOWYER
RD
ASHLEY
DR
EDEN
DORSET
CL
FIELD
VIEW
GRIMTHORPE
MARTIND

MARY S
ST
RD
DENE
RD
MILNER
RD
WAUCHOPE
RD
GATE
ACRE
RD
ROAD
ROAD
SANDPIPER
LINNET
SWALLOW
CL
ASHURST
SHERWOOD
AV

FAVERSHAM
FOX
ST
KIMBERLEY
ROBERTS
GR
MACDONALD
PARADE
SWALLOW
AV
SUNEY
SHEPPEY
POLAND
PL

Caravan
Park
LUCERNE DR
LUCERNE
DRIVE
BEACONS
FIELD
GROVE
THE
CHASE
CHANCTONBURY
CHASE
GRANGE
ST
CUMBRIAST
NIGHTINGALE AVENUE
ANTHONY
CRES
SANDEND
WW
HARTY FERRY
WW
WRAIK

6

LADYSMITH
GR
FAVERSHAM
FREEMANS
HERITAGE
CL
JAYNE
WK

ROAD
CHURCH

Caravan
Park
Caravan
Parks
Caravan
Parks
SEASALTER
LANE
LANE
THANET

A299

WA

A   B   C   D

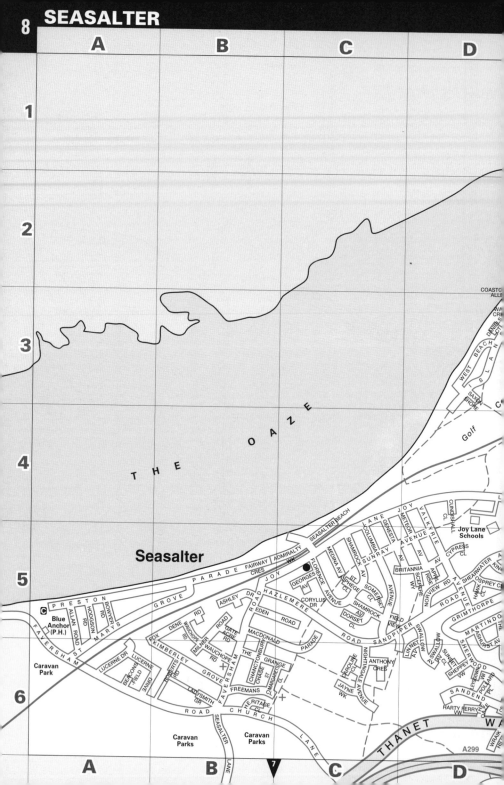

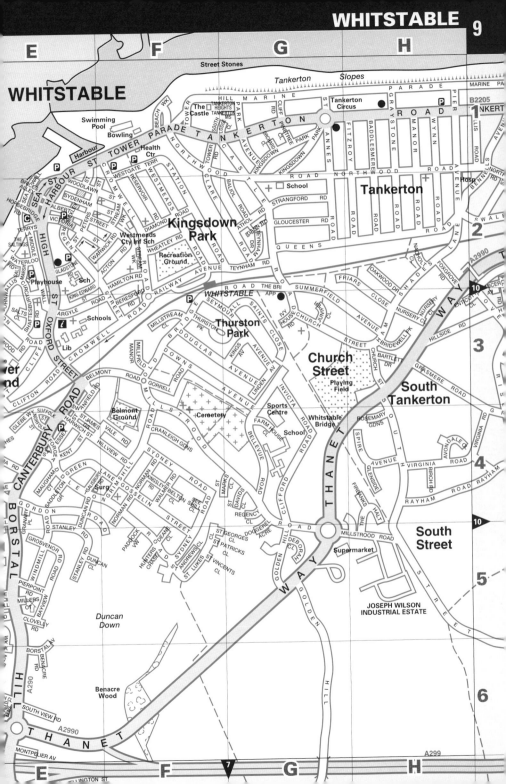

E   F   G   H

WHITSTABLE

Street Stones

Tankerton Slopes

MARINE PA

B2205

NKERT

1

Swimming Pool
Bowling
Harbour

The Castle
TANKERTON HEIGHTS
TANKERTON RD

Tankerton Circus

PARADE

PIER

MARINE

HILL

PARK

GRAYSTONE

ROAD

LUS

Health Ctr
Westgate Terr
RESERVOIR
WESTMEADS

BEACH WK
TOWER
TOWER PARADE
NORTHWOOD
CLARE
ST ANNES
PINE TREE
KINGSDOWN
INGHAM
CLIFF RD
FITZROY
BADDLESMERE
MANOR
WYNN
ROAD
AVENUE
BENNELLS
NORTH

SEA ST
HARBOUR ST
ST
HIGH ST
WOODLAWN
SYDENHAM
CROMWELL
STATION
DIAMOND
STREAM
BALUCH
KINGSDOWN
ATHOL
ROAD
NORTHWOOD
ROAD
Hosp
AVENUE

Tankerton

School
STRANGFORD   RD
GLOUCESTER   RD

SWALE

A2990

2

WHITSTABLE

C
TERRYS
THE SALTINGS
ALBERT ST
PETERS STREET
VICTORIA
GLADSTONE
Sch
WARWICK
ACTON
Westmeads Cty Inf Sch
WHEATLEY RD
Recreation Ground

Kingsdown Park

ROAD
TEYNHAM
ROAD

QUEENS
ROAD

NICHOLLS
OAKWOOD DR
FOXGROVE
A2990

10

WATERLOO
CORNWALLIS CIRCUS
SALTS
MIDDLE WALL
Playhouse
KING EDWARD
REGENT
HAMILTON RD
BERESFORD
Railway

WHITSTABLE
SEYMOUR
THURSTON PK
KINGS AV
LINDEN
Thurston Park

ROAD THE BRI
APP
SUMMERFIELD
FRIARS
CLOSE
AVENUE
BRIDEWELL PK
NURSERY
CL
STREET
HADD
GRASMERE

3

OXFORD STREET
Lib
CROMWELL
MILLSTREAM CL
MILLFIELD MANOR
ROAD
DOUGLAS
DOWNS
SAINTS CLOSE
AVENUE
INVICTA
CHURCH
CHURCH
BARTLETT
DR
HILLSIDE

Church Street

South Tankerton

CLIFTON
ROAD
BELMONT
ROAD
GORRELL
ROAD
AVENUE
IVY HOUSE
AP
Cemetery
Sports Centre
FARM HOUSE
BELLEVUE
Whitstable Bridge
School
Playing Field
SPIRE
ROSEMARY GDNS

ST JAMES
HARWICH ST
VALE RD
CRANLEIGH GDNS
ST MARKS
ST DAVIDS
ROAD
AVENUE
GLENSIDE
FIRBANKS
VIRGINIA
AVONDALE RD
BIRCH RD
Virginia Road

4

GLEBE WY
SUFFOLK
NORFOLK
ESSEX
KENT
GREEN
HILLVIEW
SYDNEY
ROAD
WALMELTON CL
ST GEORGES
REGENCY
DOGGEREL ACRE
CLIFFORD ROAD
RAYHAM
RAYHAM

CANTERBURY ROAD
FANFIELD
BELMONT Ground
MAUGHAM
SADDLETON GT
SAUNDERS LANE
NGHTINGALE HILL
NORMAN RD
MELLIN
STREET
ST ANDREWS CL
ST LUKES
ST VINCENTS CL
ROAD
SUPERMARKET

South Street

BORSTAL HILL
GORDON PL
STANLEY
DUNCAN RD
STANLEY RD
PADDOCK WY
HUNTERS CHASE
SYDNEY
ST PATRICKS
GOLDEN HILL
DEBORA RD
MILLSTROOD ROAD

10

WAY

THANET

5

GROSVENOR
WINDMILL
RD
PIERPOINT RD
BAYVIEW
MILLERS CT
CLOVELLY RD
SOUTH VIEW RD

Duncan Down

GOLDEN HILL

JOSEPH WILSON INDUSTRIAL ESTATE

6

BORSTAL AV
BENACRE RD

Benacre Wood

STREET

A2990
THANET

MONTPELIER AV

A299

E   F   G   H

7

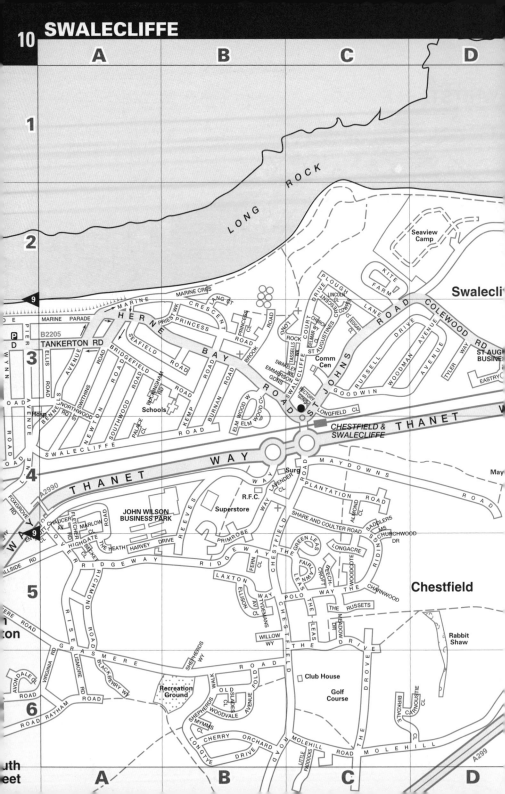

Swalecli

Chestfield

LONG ROCK

Seaview Camp

KITE FARM

PLOUGH LANE

COLEWOOD RD

ST AUG BUSINE

EASTRY

MARINE CRES

LANG CT

CRESCENT

MARINE

HERNE BAY ROAD

MARINE PARADE

B2205

TANKERTON RD

PIER

PRIEST WK

PRINCESS ROAD

PRINCESS

BROOK

LONG ROCK

CRESCENT

CHURCH ST

ST AUGUSTINES

LINCOLN

DRIVE

DELMAR WY

JOHNS ROAD

RUSSELL DRIVE

WOODMAN AVENUE

AVENUE

TYLER WAY

SEAFIELD ROAD

BRIDGEFIELD ROAD

SOUTHWOOD ROAD

BUCKINGHAM RD

KEMP ROAD

BURNAN ROAD

ELM WOOD W

ELM WOOD CL

SWALECLIFFE AVENUE

EMMERSON GDNS

TASSELLS

COURT

Comm Cen

LONGFIELD CL

GOODWIN

Schools

PALACE CL

SWALECLIFFE AVENUE

NEWTON RD

NORTHWOOD RD

WITHINS

BINNS

ELLIS ROAD

AVENUE

Hosp

CHESTFIELD & SWALECLIFFE

THANET

May

FOXGROVE RD

A2990

THANET WAY

Surg

R.F.C.

Superstore

JOHN WILSON BUSINESS PARK

LAVENDER CL

WAY

MAYDOWNS ROAD

PLANTATION ROAD

ALMOND CL

SADDLERS

CHURCHWOOD DR

MS

RIDING

Rabbit Shaw

CHAUCER AV

FLETCHER RD

MARLOW

HIGHGATE

THE HEATH

HARVEY DRIVE

REEVES

RIDGE WAY

FERN CL

SHARE AND COULTER ROAD

LONGACRE

BEECH

WOODCOTE

GREEN LEAS

FAIRWAY

CROFT

CHARNWOOD

THE RUSSETS

RIDGEWAY

RICHMOND ROAD

RISE

GRASMERE

LAXTON WAY

ELLISON AV CL

W TYDEMANS AV CL

WILLOW WY

POLO WAY

CHESTFIELD ROAD

THE LEAS

THE LEAS

MEADOW DR

THE DRIVE

Chestfield

VIRGINIA RD

LISMORE ROAD

BLACKBERRY WY

Recreation Ground

SHEPHERDS WY

WALK

SHEPHERDS WY

MYMMS CL

WOODVALE

OLD SLADE

ROAD

AVENUE

FOLD

Club House

Golf Course

THE DROVE

BIRKDALE CL

CARNOUSTIE CL

AVONDALE CL

ROAD

RAYHAM ROAD

CHERRY ORCHARD DRIVE

LONGTYE

MOLEHILL ROAD

LITTLE PADDOCKS

MOLEHILL ROAD

A299

uth eet

A   B   C   D

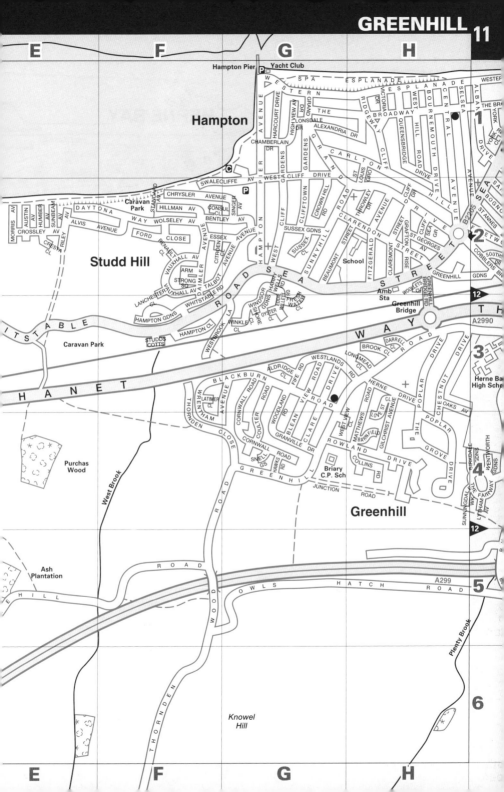

E   F   G   H

Hampton Pier   Yacht Club

Hampton

WESTERN AVENUE
WEST SPA ESPLANADE
ESPLANADE WEST
ESPLANADE
WESTER
ALBAN
THE BRO
YORK
PARK
DRIVE

HARCOURT DRIVE
HIGHVIEW AV
LONSDALE
CHAMBERLAIN DR
THE BROADWAY
RIDGEWAY DR
VICTORIA
CLIFF HILL
BOURNEMOUTH DRIVE
CENTRAL AV
SELSEA AV
1

ALEXANDRA DR
QUEENSBRIDGE
SWALECLIFFE AV
WEST CLIFF GARDENS
GRAND DRIVE
CARLTON ROAD
CLIFF AVENUE
ST ANNES

CHRYSLER AVENUE
HILLMAN AV
CONSUL CL
BENTLEY
CITROEN
CLIFFTOWN GARDENS
CROWN HILL RD
ST LOUIS GRO
THROWLEY DR
GRAFTON ROAD
ST SEA GR
GREENHILL
COBBLERS
SOUTH
BR
GDNS

Studd Hill

MORRIS AV
AUSTIN
HUMBER
SUNBEAM
DAYTONA
CRESTA CL
ALVIS AVENUE
CROSSLEY AV
RILEY
WAY
WOLSELEY AV
FORD CLOSE
RENAULT
ESSEX AVENUE
SINGER
Caravan Park

VAUXHALL AV
DAIMLER AVENUE
STRONG SQ
ARM
TALBOT
LANCHESTER CL
VAUXHALL AV
WHITSTABLE RD
HAMPTON GDNS
HAMPTON CL
WINKLES CL
WEST CLIFF
CL
SUSSEX GDNS
SUSSEX CL
SUNNYHILL AV
BEAUMONT
CLAREMONT
CLARENDON STREET
FITZGERALD
ST GEORGES
GRAFTON STREET RISE
STREET
School

Amb Sta
WOOGLETS CL
Greenhill Bridge
GREENHILL BRIDGE RD

Caravan Park
STUDDS COTTS
WESTBROOK ROAD
HAMPTON CL
WINDSOR DR
OYSTER
HOLLY
WATTS CL
WELLS
EDENS
FRESH WATER CL
ROAD SEA WAY

WHITSTABLE
THANET WAY
A2990
12

BLACKBURN AVENUE
ALDRIDGE CL
FIFE RD
WESTLANDS ROAD
BROOK CL
DARRELL CL
LONGMEAD RD
POPLAR DRIVE
CHESTNUT DRIVE
POPLAR DRIVE
3

THORNDEN CLOSE
WRENTHAM AVENUE
CORNWALL ROAD
COULTER ROAD
WOODLAND ROAD
BLEAN VIEW ROAD
CLARE DRIVE
WEST VIEW
HERNE ROAD
MATTHEWS
ST JOHNS
GILCHRIST AVENUE
BARNFIELD
HERNE
OAKS AV
THE GROVE
POPLAR DRIVE
Herne Ba
High Sch

GREENHILL ROAD
CORNWALL ROAD
SNELL
HAWKS RD
GRANVILLE DR
ROWLAND
COLLINS DR
Briary C.P. Sch
WENTWORTH GDNS
SUNNINGDALE
WENTWORTH
THE FAIRWAY
LYTHAM WY
4

Purchas Wood
West Brook

JUNCTION ROAD

Greenhill

12

Ash Plantation
ROAD
WOOD OWLS HATCH ROAD
A299
5

WOOD ROAD
Plenty Brook

Knowel Hill
6

E   F   G   H

ITSTABLE

HANET

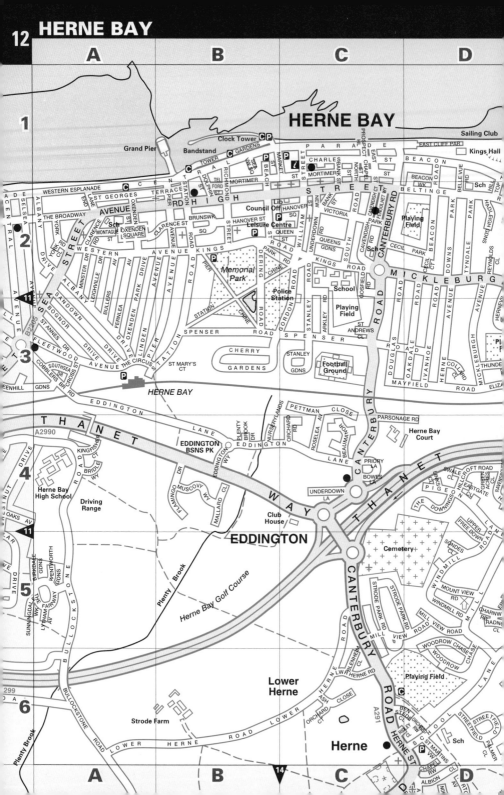

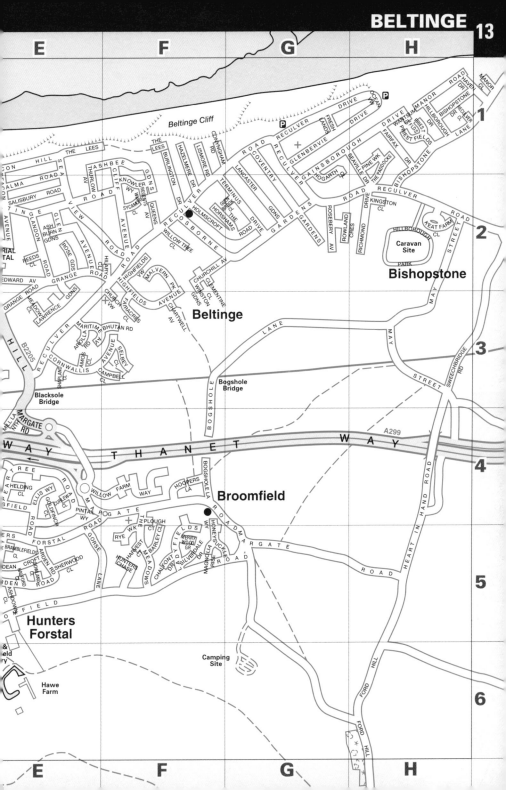

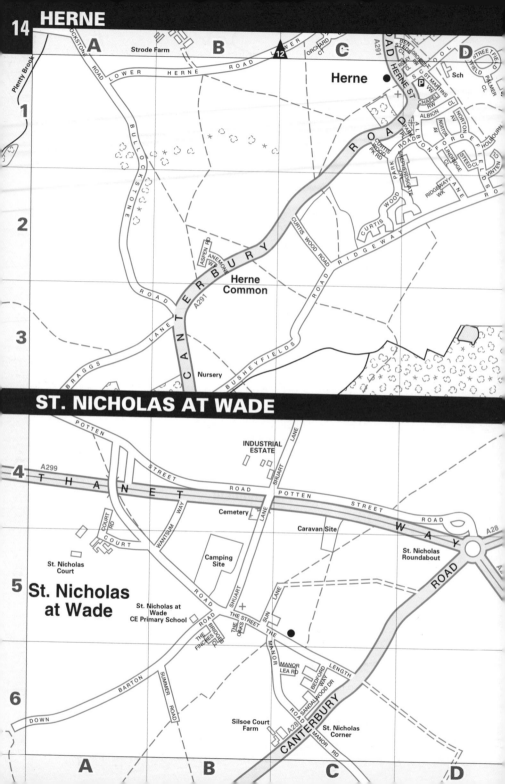

HERNE

14

A — DOCKSTONE ROAD — B — Strode Farm — ▲ 12 — ORCHARD CT — C — A291 — HERNE ST — D

LOWER HERNE ROAD — Herne ● — STREET FIELD — PALMER CL — Sch

Plenty Brook

BULLOCKSTONE — ROAD — ALBION — CHAPEL RW — ALBION — NORTON AV — RG CL — LINDRIDGE — STEED — HOLBOURN — VINTEN

1

PARK — CURTIS WOOD PK RD — WOOD — PARK — RIDGEWAY WK

2

ASPEN RD — ANEMONE WY — CANTERBURY — ROAD — A291 — CURTIS WOOD ROAD — ROAD — CURTIS WOOD ROAD — RIDGEWAY

Herne Common

3

LANE — CANTERBURY — Nursery — BUSHEYFIELDS — BRAGGS

ST. NICHOLAS AT WADE

POTTEN

4 — A299 — T H A N E T — STREET — ROAD — SHUART LANE — POTTEN — STREET — ROAD — WAY — A28

INDUSTRIAL ESTATE

Cemetery

Caravan Site — St. Nicholas Roundabout

COURT RD — WANTSUM WAY — LANE — ROAD

5 — St. Nicholas Court — Camping Site — St. Nicholas at Wade CE Primary School — SUN LANE — THE STREET — ROAD

St. Nicholas at Wade

ROAD — THE BRIDGES — THE FINCHES CL — OAKS — THE STREET — THE MANOR

MANOR LEA RD — BEDFORD WAY — LENGTH

6 — BARTON — SUMMER — ROAD — ROAD — SANDALWOOD DR — CANTERBURY — A28 — MANOR RD

DOWN — Silsoe Court Farm — St. Nicholas Corner

A — B — C — D

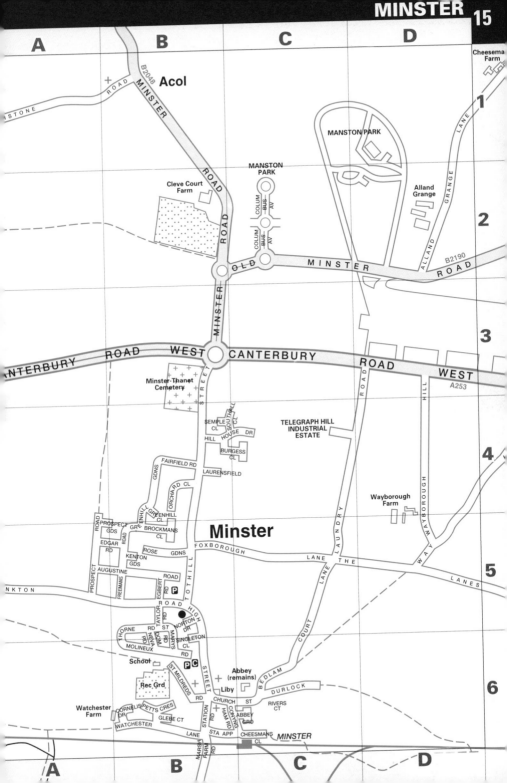

A   B   C   D

Cheesema
Farm

Acol

B2048

MINSTER

ROAD

STONE
ROAD

1

MANSTON PARK

Alland
Grange

GRANGE LANE

MANSTON
PARK

Cleve Court
Farm

COLUM - BUS - AV

COLUM - BUS - AV

MINSTER

ROAD

B2190

OLD   MINSTER   ROAD

ALLAND

ROAD

2

MINSTER

3

CANTERBURY   ROAD   WEST   CANTERBURY   ROAD   WEST

A253

Minster-Thanet
Cemetery

STREET

ROAD

HILL   WAYBOROUGH

TELEGRAPH HILL
INDUSTRIAL
ESTATE

SEMPLE
CL

SOUTHALL CL

HILL   HOUSE   DR

BURGESS
CL

4

FAIRFIELD RD

LAURENSFIELD

GDNS

ORCHARD CL

Wayborough
Farm

Minster

GREENHILL
CL

GRE...
ROAD

BROCKMANS
CL

PROSPECT
GDS

ROAD

EDGAR
RD

ROSE   GDNS

FOXBOROUGH

LANE

THE   LANES

5

KENTON
GDS

LANE

LAUNDRY

PROSPECT

AUGUSTINE

FREEMANS

EGBERT
RD

ROAD

P

TOTHILL

WAY   WAYBOROUGH

COURT   LANE

THORNE

TAYLOR
RD

ST
MARYS

NEWNHAM
RD

SINGLETON
CL

HIGH   ROAD

NORTON
DR

MOLINEUX

School   P   C

Rec Grd

ST MILDREDS

Abbey
(remains)

ST

STREET

BEDLAM

DURLOCK

RIVERS
CT

6

Watchester
Farm

CORNELIS
DR

PETTS CRES

GLEBE CT

Liby

CHURCH

ABBEY
GRD

WATCHESTER

STATION   RD

MARSH FARM RD

STA APP

CHEESMANS
CL

MINSTER

NKTON

LANE

A   B   C   D

A **B** **C** **D**

1

2

Greenham Bay

CLIFF ROAD

MINNIS BAY

Paddling Pool

THE PARADE

ANNA PARK

SEA VIEW AV

HEREWARD AV

HAROLD ROAD

ALFRED ROAD

ETHELBERT RD

WALTER RD

SEA VIEW ROAD

GRENVILLE GDNS

BERKELEY RD

SEMAPHORE RD

HERSCHELL RD

DALE

DINGER SP

BERESFORD

AVENUE

DARWIN RD

BEACH

3 Wantsum Walk

C P

THE HENGIST RD

QUEENS RD

KINGS AVENUE

CANUTE RD

ARTHUR RD

VIKING CL

MANNIS

DANEHORSA RD

EGBERT RD

RECULVER ROAD

ST MILDREDS RD

GALLWEY AV

NELSON CT

CUNNINGHAM CRES

DUNCAN DR

GRENHAM

GREEN

GATE

HUNTING

HUNTING GATE

HUNTINGTON CT

YELL RD

ROSSETTI RD

BIRCHINGTON

DARYNGTON AV

DANE ROAD

INGOLDSBY ROAD

ROAD

MANNIS ROAD

GORE END

GORDON SQ

KENT GDNS

RUTLAND GDNS

SUSSEX GDNS

LINCOLN GDNS

DORSET GDNS

SANDLES RD

KINGS RD

PROSPECT

SURREY

Gore End Farm

4 **Birchington**

DEVON

ESSEX

LANCASTER

MANOR GARDENS

MILL LA

MILL ROW

CANTERB

QUEX

5

BROADLEY AV

KING

NOTTINGH RD

SHERWOOD

6 Upper Hale

Great Brooksend Farm

Little Brooksend Farm

Brooks End

ROAD

College Farm

CRISPE

SEAMARK ROAD

A28

CANTERBURY ROAD

A **B** **C** **D**

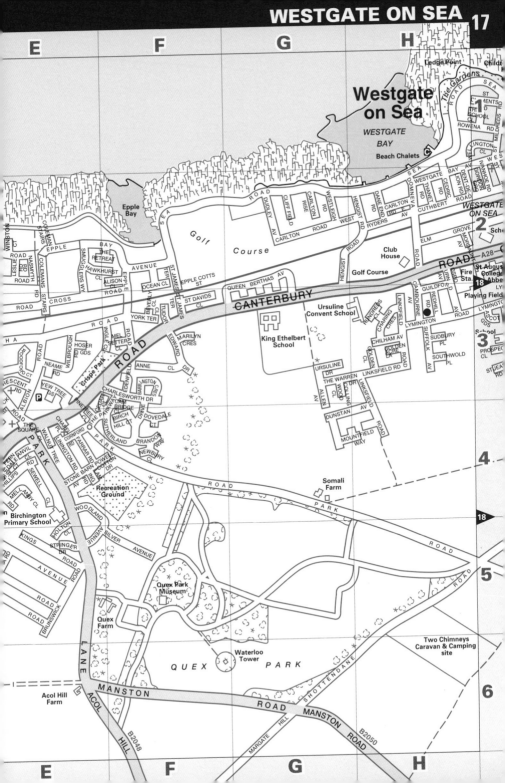

E F G H

Ledge Point   Childs

Westgate
on Sea

THE GARDENS ROAD
MENTS
THE SCHOOL
ST
GD
ROWENA
MILDREDS AV
S MILDREDS RD

WESTGATE
BAY

Beach Chalets

SEA

INGTON CL
WHIGO RD
THANET RD
OXENDEN RD
WES

WESTGATE
ON SEA

Sch

Epple
Bay

Golf
Course

ROAD
DUDLEY
CLIFF FIELD
CARLTON RISE
CARLTON RD
WESTLEIGH RD
HENGIST RD
WEST
DANE END
DOMNEY
THANET RD
CEDRIC RD
ION RD
CARLTON AV
CUTHBERT

WESTGATE
AV
BAY
RYDERS
CARLTON ROAD
WEST
HENGIST RD
RD
ELM   GROVE
MORDEN
AV

Club
House

Golf Course

ROAD — A28 —

St Augus
College
Abbe

WINSTON RD
LESLIE RD
NASMYTH RD
COLEMANS WY
COLEMAN STAIRS ROAD
EPPLE
BAY
THE RETREAT
HAWKHURST CL
ALISON RD
EPPLE
SMUGGLERS WY
OCEAN CL
AVENUE
TERN
TUDOR TER
ST JAMES ST
ST JAMES TER
EPPLE COTTS
ST DAVIDS CL
BEVERLY
ROAD

QUEEN BERTHAS AV

URN
CAMBOURNE
GUILDFORD

Fire
Sta.

LYMINGTON
ST AUG CL
LYMINGTON
18

Playing Field

ROAD
CROSS
STAIRS ROAD
YORK TER

ROAD

CANTERBURY

Ursuline
Convent School

KINGREN
CHARING CRES
LINKSFIELD AV
REDHILL
SUFFOLK
LYMINGTON
SUDBURY PL
SOUTHWOLD PL

School

PROSPECT
CL
ST HEAD RD

H A

CRESCENT
GLOSTON CT
ALBION RD
THE SQUARE
P
YEW TREE
NEAME RD
HOSER RD
INGS
MEL ST
GDS
WROUGHT
ANNE CL

MARILYN CRES
EDWARD
CL DR

Crispe Park

KING ETHELBERT
ROAD

King Ethelbert
School

URSULINE DR

CHILHAM AV
GOLDEN
ACRE
GOLDEN RD
LINKSFIELD RD

SUFFOLK

3

FERN
SQUARE RD
PROSPECT RD
PHILLIPS
CHAPEL
COTT
LLINGTON RD
WALNUT TREE
FARRAR RD
THE PARK
INE TREE
PARK
EDENFIELD
NGTON CRES
CHARLESWORTH DR
ROAD BRIDGE
BIRCH HILL CT
SUTHERLAND
DOVEDALE
BRANDON WAY
NEWBURY CL

THE WARREN
WOOD
LING
ALLEN AV

LINKSFIELD RD

DUNSTAN AV

ROAD

MOUNTFIELD WAY

4

18

MEL
ANDY CL
SEWELL RD
Birchington
Primary School
STONE BARN
AV
POWELL
COPELAND RD
Recreation
Ground
WOODLAND
BOLTON CL

ROAD

Somali
Farm

PARK

ROAD

KINGS
AVENUE
STRINGER DR
ROAD
SILVER
AVENUE

AVENUE

5

AVENUE
ROAD
BRUNSWICK RD
ROAD

Quex Park
Museum

Quex
Farm

ROAD

Two Chimneys
Caravan & Camping
site

Acol Hill
Farm
ACOL HILL
B2048
MANSTON
LANE
ROAD

QUEX

Waterloo
Tower

PARK

SHOTTENDANE

MANSTON   ROAD   B2050

MARGATE HILL

6

E F G H

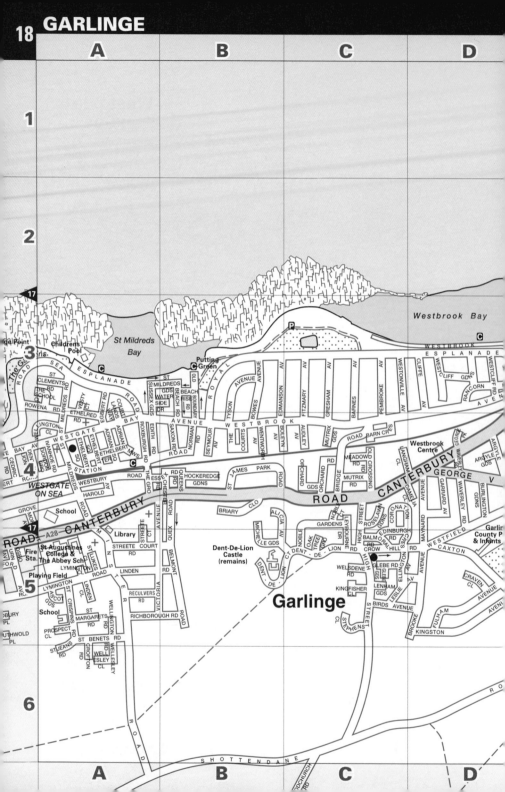

Westbrook Bay

St Mildreds Bay

Childrens Pool

Putting Green

WESTBROOK ESPLANADE

ESPLANADE

Garlinge

Dent-De-Lion Castle (remains)

Westbrook Centre

St Augustines College & The Abbey Sch

Library

Fire Sta.

School

School

Playing Field

Garlinge County P & Infants

CANTERBURY ROAD

SHOTTENDANE ROAD

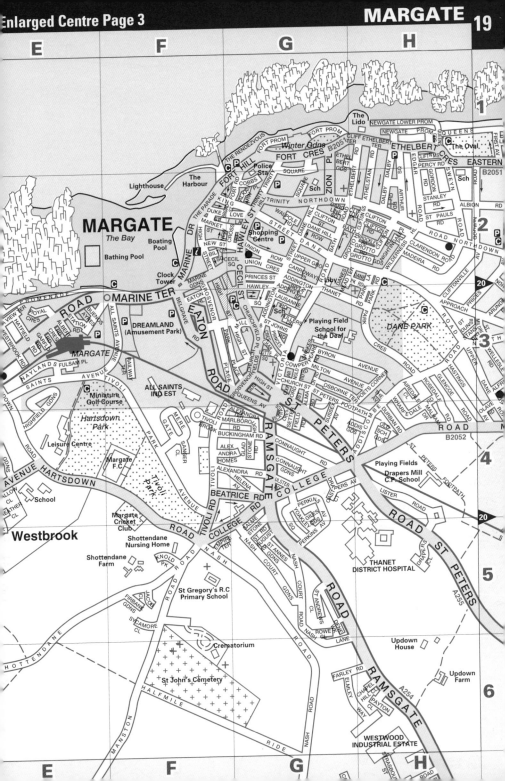

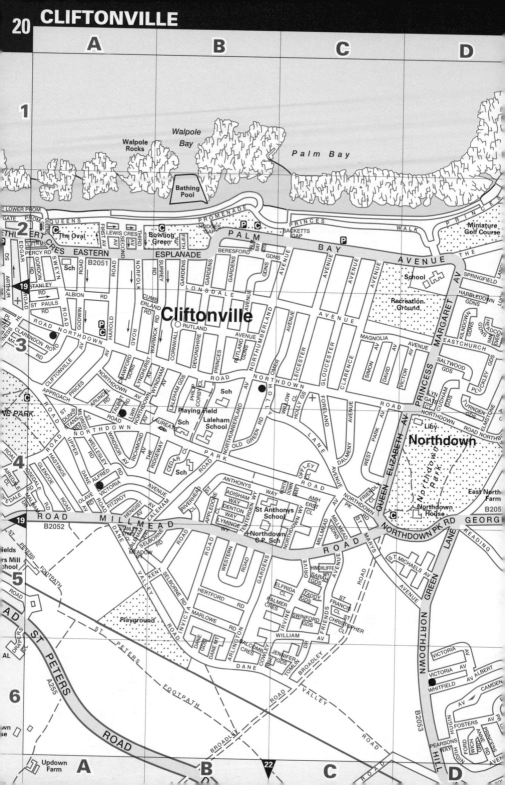

E   F   G   H

1

RENESS POINT

2

Botany Bay

W
RIDINGS
FORENESS ROAD
MARINE
DRIVE
SECOND AV
AVENUE
Whiteness

Kingsgate Bay

3

KHOLT
SPELD GS
HURST GDNS
CHURCH
HALSTEAD GDNS
HURST GDNS
LAMBER HURST WAY
BUCK HURST DR
YARD
EYNS FORD CL
PENS HURST CL
COPPERHURST WK
SANDHURST
NYE DALKHAM
WYE CL
TEYNHAM CL
ALKHAM CL
FIELD RD
CHAT CL
LOCK
AV
DOLPHIN CL
COLETTE CL
AVENUE

Captain Digby Inn

KINGSGATE BAY RD
ROAD
Kingsgate Castle
Hackemdown Point

4

BOTANY
WESTER HAM
BROMFIELD CRES
PERCY
FIRST AV
FITZROY AV
FITZROY
KINGSGATE
CAPEL
WHITENESS TERN
WOODLAND OAKRIDGE
ROAD
CONVENT

Kingsgate
Golf Course

JOSS GAP ROAD
NTH FORELAND

Joss Bay

HILL ROAD
WHITENESS ROAD
GEORGE HILL ROAD

North Foreland Golf Course
AVENUE
C P

5

Club House
Kingsgate College
ROSETOWER CT
LEBRYN GDNS
CONVENT ROAD
Reading Street
Convalescent Home

North Foreland Lighthouse

CRESCENT RD
NTH FORELAND
AVENUE
PROMENADE

6

GRAFTON
AFGHAN RD
READING RD
MOCKETT DR
CORONATION CL
LINK RD
BALLIOL RD
CHURCHFIELD
ASTOR
TY SQ
ELMWOOD CL
STREET
ELMWOOD
CEDAR CL
GREEN
THE OAKS
NORTHCLIFFE GDNS
THE PADDOCKS
ROAD
ELMWOOD
Elmwood Farm
Convalescent Home
College
NORTH FORELAND ROAD
NORTH FORELAND AVENUE
ANNES RD
B2052
CLIFF ROAD
PROMENADE
Hope Point

School
FIG TREE RD
GUY CL
KING FRANCIS
LANTHURNE

23

E   F   G   H

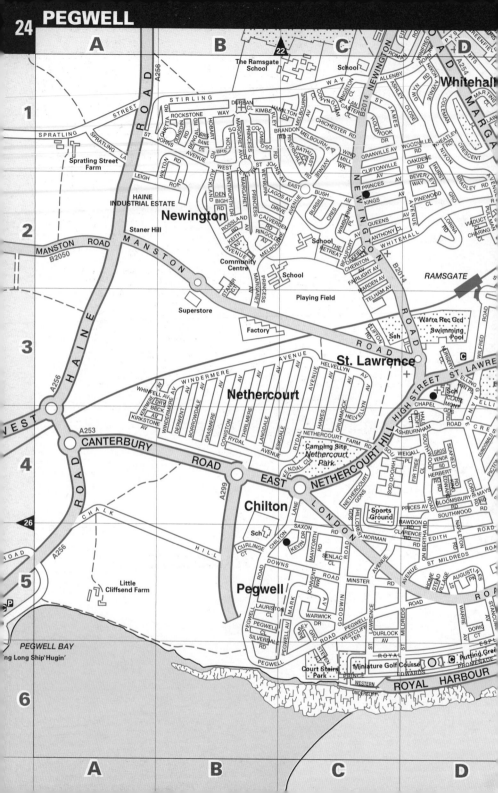

A B C D

1

The Ramsgate School

School

Whitehall

MARGA

SPRATLING

Spratling Street Farm

STIRLING

ROCKSTONE

DURBAN

HAMILTON

CHICHESTER RD

Allenby

ASHLEY CLOSE

JAMES

ROMAN

NEWINGTON

A2014

2

HAINE INDUSTRIAL ESTATE

Newington

Staner Hill

MANSTON ROAD
B2050

MANSTON ROAD

Community Centre

WENTWORTH

PRINCESS

MARGARET AV

ROSSLAND

KEITH AVENUE

MELBOU

CALVERDEN

RINGOLD

School

School

Playing Field

Granville Av

CLIFTONVILLE

OAKDENE

Princes

AV

Kings

Queens

School

RETREAT

BEAUFORT

CHERITON

FAIRLIGHT AV

MARDEN AV

TELHAM AV

WHITEHALL

BEVERLEY WAY

PINEWOOD CL

VIADUCT

CHARING CL

RAMSGATE

3

Superstore

Staner Ct

Factory

WINDERMERE

AVENUE

HELVELLYN

HELVELLYN

CLIFTON

Seh

ROAD

ROAD

Warre Rec Grd

Swimming Pool

NURSERY

St. Lawrence

St. Lawre

CL

Sch

CLARE MONT

Chapel

HALL

HIGH STREET

4

WEST
ROAD

A256

CANTERBURY

A253

ROAD

A299

CHALK

ROAD EAST

WINDERMERE

DERWENT

BORROWDALE

GRASMERE

CONISTON

RYDAL

THIRLMERE

LANGDALE

ESKDALE

RYDAL

KENDAL

HAWES

GRUMMOCK

HELVELLYN

AVENUE

Nethercourt

Camping Site
Nethercourt Park

NETHERCOURT FARM

NETHERCOURT GDNS

NETHERCOURT HILL

LONDON

Sports Ground

ASHBURNHAM

SOUTHWOOD

WEIGALL

FIR TREE

HERBERT

BLOOMSBURY

SOUTHWOOD

RAWDON

CLARENCE

NORMAN

ST MILDREDS

GROS

SEAFIELD

EDWARD

LORNE

MAYS

GDS

PRICES AV

NAPLETON

EDITH

ROAD

26

A256

5

Chilton

Pegwell

Sch

CURLINGE CT

KEVIN DR

CHILTON

SAXON

MAYFORTH

SENLAC CL

DOWNS

CONVENT

WK

WARWICK

DR

LAURISTON CL

PEGWELL

SILVERDALE

PEGWELL AV

MARK

ABBEY

STEVEN

GOODWIN

ROAD

MINSTER

WESTCLIFF TER

DURLOCK

AV

ST LAWRENCE

ROYAL

ST MILDREDS

AUGUSTINES

ROAD

Miniature Golf Course

Putting Green

PROMENADE

ESPL

6

PEGWELL BAY

ng Long Ship 'Hugin'

Court Stairs Park

PRINCE

WESTERN

UNDERCLIFF

ROYAL HARBOUR

A B C D

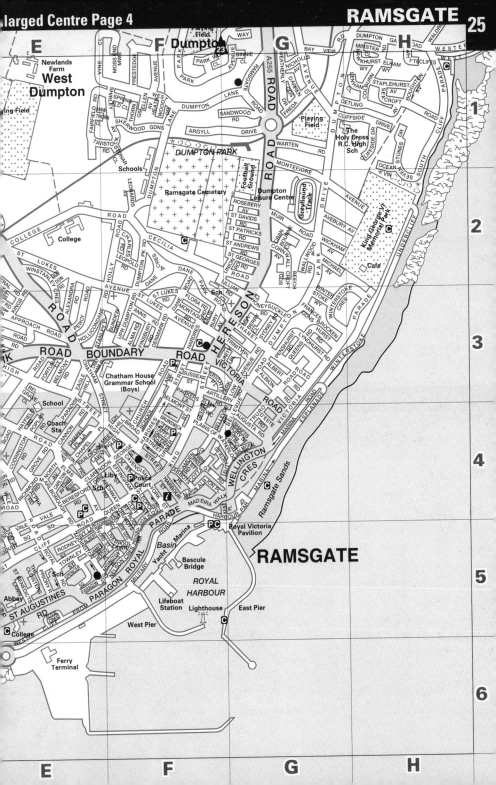

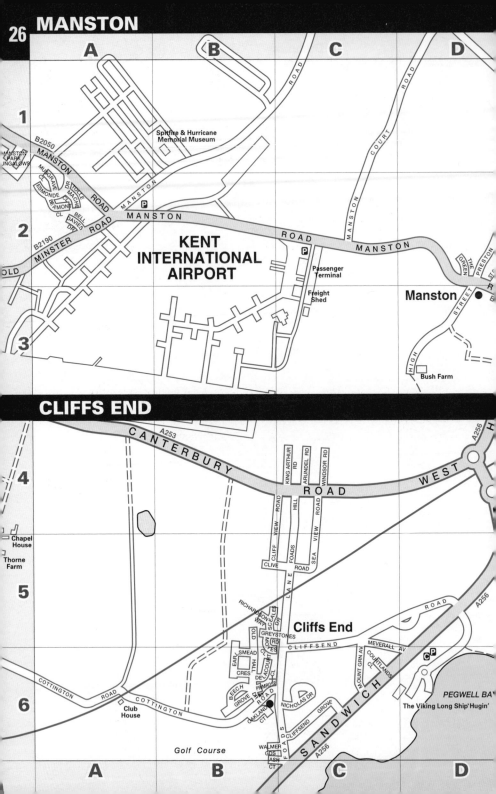

MANSTON

- A B C D
- **1**
- Spitfire & Hurricane Memorial Museum
- B2050 MANSTON
- MANSTON PARK BUNGALOWS
- MUSGRAVE RD
- IDDLE
- ESMONDE
- DE MACE
- AMON CL
- BELL
- DAVIES DR
- **2** B2190 MINSTER ROAD
- MANSTON ROAD
- MANSTON ROAD MANSTON
- OLD
- **KENT INTERNATIONAL AIRPORT**
- Passenger Terminal
- Freight Shed
- MANSTON COURT ROAD
- **Manston**
- THE GREEN
- PRESTON R
- HIGH STREET
- **3**
- Bush Farm

CLIFFS END

- A253 CANTERBURY ROAD
- A256 H
- WEST
- **4**
- KING ARTHUR RD
- ARUNDEL RD
- WINDSOR RD
- ROAD
- HILL
- CLIFF VIEW ROAD
- SEA VIEW ROAD
- FOADS ROAD
- Chapel House
- Thorne Farm
- CLIVE
- **5**
- RICHARDSON WAY
- SCEALES DR
- OLD COURT CL
- LOW COURT YES
- GREYSTONES
- **Cliffs End**
- A256 ROAD
- A256
- EARL SMEAD HALL CRES
- DEV
- PRIMROSE
- CLIFFSEND
- MEVERALL AV
- COURTLANDS CL.
- MOUNT GRN AV
- GP
- ROAD
- BEECH GROVE
- OAKLAND CT
- NICHOLAS DR
- CLEFSEND GROVE
- **6** COTTINGTON ROAD
- COTTINGTON ROAD
- SANDWICH
- **PEGWELL BAY**
- The Viking Long Ship 'Hugin'
- Club House
- WALMER GDS
- ASH CT
- FOADS
- A256
- *Golf Course*
- A B C D

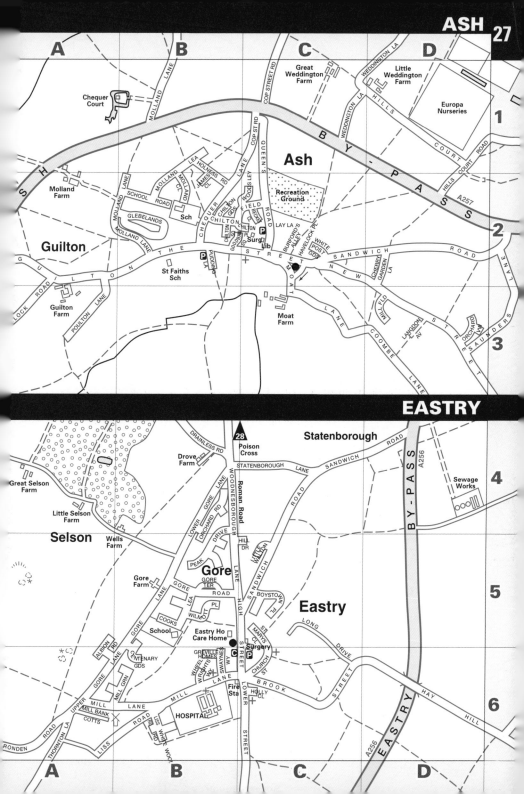

ASH (top map)

A B C D

1

Chequer Court

Great Weddington Farm

Little Weddington Farm

Europa Nurseries

WEDDINGTON LA

HILLS

MOLLAND LANE

COP STREET RD

BY-PASS

HILLS COURT ROAD

A257

ROAD

Ash

Recreation Ground

Molland Farm

SCHOOL ROAD

MOLLAND LANE

GLEBELANDS

MOLLAND CL

MOLLAND LANE

LEFT HOLNESS RD

JAMES CL

Sch

CHEQUER

CHILTON

CHILTON GDS

CHILTON

GOODWIN

FIELD

WOODSIDE

QUEEN'S

LANE

BERRY

ROAD

LAY LA

Surg
Lib
P

BURFORD'S ALLEY

HAVELOCK PL

WHITE POST GDS

SANDWICH ROAD

CHERRY GARDEN LA

LANE

Guilton

THE

Guilton Farm

St Faiths Sch
P

PUDDING

MOAT

NEW

MILL FLD

LANGDON AV

STREET

ORCHARD CL

GULLOCK ROAD

POULTON LANE

Moat Farm

COOMBE LANE

SAUNDERS LANE

2

3

EASTRY (bottom map)

A B C D

4

Great Selson Farm

Little Selson Farm

Selson

Wells Farm

Drove Farm

DRAINLESS RD

28
Poison Cross

Statenborough

STATENBOROUGH LANE

SANDWICH ROAD

ROAD

BY-PASS

A256

Sewage Works

LOWER GORE LANE

ORCHARD RD

GORE LANE

DRIVE

WOODNESBOROUGH

Roman Road

HILL DR

WILTON

SANDWICH

5

Gore Farm

PEAK

Gore

GORE TER

GORE ROAD

LEA

WILMOT PL

LANE

HIGH

BOYSTOWN PL

Eastry

LONG DRIVE

STREET

GORE LANE

School

COOKS

Eastry Ho Care Home

C
Surgery
P

ST MARYS CL

CHURCH ST

BROOK

HAY HILL

EASTRY

A256

ALBION RD

CENTENARY GDS

GREVILLE HOMES

WHEEL WRIGHTS LANE

SWAYNES YM

STREET

Fire Sta

HOLLY CL

LOWER STREET

6

MILL GRN

UPPER MILL RD

COTTS

MILL BANK

LANE

MILL ROAD

LISS ROAD

LISS

WHITE WOOD

HOSPITAL

THORNTON LA

RONDEN ROAD

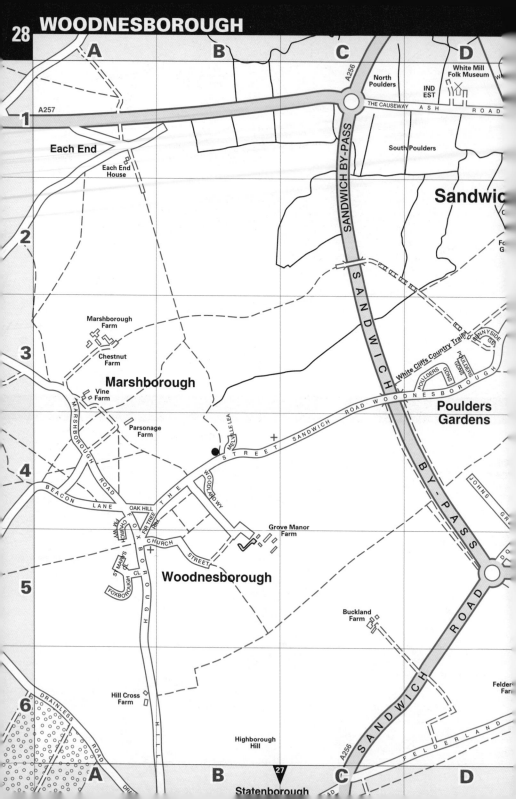

A   B   C   D

1

A257

Each End

Each End House

SANDWICH BY-PASS

A256

North Poulders

South Poulders

THE CAUSEWAY   A S H   R O A D

IND EST

White Mill Folk Museum

Sandwic

2

Marshborough Farm

Chestnut Farm

Marshborough

Vine Farm

3

SANNYSIDE GS

White Cliffs Country Trail

POULDERS GDNS

POULDERS GDNS

WOODNESBOROUGH

Fo G

Parsonage Farm

MARSHBOROUGH ROAD

MELVILLE LEA

S T R E E T

SANDWICH ROAD WOODNESBOROUGH

Poulders Gardens

4

BEACON LANE

OAK HILL

T H E

F O X B O R O U G H   H I L L

CHURCH RD

WOODLAND WY

FIR TREE RD

Grove Manor Farm

JOHNS GR

BY - PASS

5

CHURCH STREET

ST MARYS CL

FOXBOROUGH

Woodnesborough

Buckland Farm

SANDWICH ROAD

6

DRAINLESS ROAD

Hill Cross Farm

H I L L

Highborough Hill

A256

FELDERLAND

Felder Far

A   B   C   D

27
Statenborough

E   F   G   H

Stonar Lake

CRYSTAL BUSINESS CENTRE

1

Nature Reserve

Gazen Salts Recreation Ground

STONAR GDNS

RAMSGATE ROAD

STONAR CL

STONAR

ROAD

The King's House

Manwood Court

Sch

PARADISE ROW

MULBERRY

VIC RD

BROWNING ST

MARKET ST

HARNET

RED COW

ST PETERS

AYSHER

LITTLE

HIGH ST

The Barbican

River

SANDWICH INDUSTRIAL ESTATE

The New Cut

North Stream

recreation Ground

HOSP

THE QUAY

Fisher Gate

The Bulwark

The Salutation

Stour

White Cliffs Country Trail

The Guildhall

DELF STREET

UPR STRAND STREET

FISHER ST

STRAND

MOAT SOLE

CATTLE MKT

WHITEFRIARS MDW

NEW

KING ST

ST MARYS

WATER

SHORT ST

CHAIN

HOGS

CNR

Rope Walk

Town Wall

GALLIARD ST

ST

KNIGHTRIDER STREET

Mill Wall

DOWN

Vigo

Sprong

2

Cemetery

JUBILEE RD

DIDWOOD RD

FORDWICH

Rec Grnd

NEW

DOVER

LEESE END

ST GEORGES

ELFSIDE

Playing Field

Little Sandown Farm

SANDOWN LEES

AVENUE

STS

ROAD

Pol Sta

ANDREWS

ST GEORGES

Sir Roger Manwood's School

ROAD

3

BARTS

AVENUE

HAZELWOOD MDW

DOVER ROAD

SANDWICH

Sports Ground

Sandwich County Junior School

LEES

CROSS

ROAD

4

ne ss

Sports & Leisure Centre

Sandwich Technology School

DEAL

5

58

Little Temptye

Blue Pigeons

GORETOP LANE

LANE

Temptye Farmhouse

Coventon Lane

Worth Hill

DEAL ROAD

Links Farm

Worth Cty Prim Sch

MINNIS WAY

Minnis Farm

6

Felderland

LANE

THE STREET

JUBILEE ROAD

Worth

Great Wood

A2258

CHESTNUT DR

TEMPLE WAY

E   F   G   H

A **B** **C** **D**

1

2

3

4

5

6

Police Sta
BROAD-THE GAP
LANDS IND EST
CHAPEL
GERS CL
LANE
BOURNE LODGE CL
BLEAN
A290
WOODVILLE
CHESTNUT AV
SCHOOL LANE
HILL RD
Reservoir (Covered)
P
Hall
Rec Grd
THE GREEN
BOY-ARDS
TYLER
HILL
Hothe Court Farm
Blean
WESTFIELD
COMMON BLEAN
MOUNT PLEASANT
St. Cosmos & St. Damian in the Blean
Hillside Farm
Luckett's Farm
HILL TILE KILN HILL
Hare & Hounds PH
HILL
Blean Cty Prim Sch
UNIVERSITY OF KE
AT CANTERBUR
WHITSTABLE
PARK
PURCHAS CT
LYPEATT CT
WOOD
Canterbury Bsns Sch
R&D Centre
Laboratorie
ELLENDEN CT
BISHOPDEN CT
THORNDEN CT
FARTHINGS CT
WOODLAND
Sports Centre
GRIMSHILL CT
CLOWES CT
MARLEY CT
DENSTEAD CT
HOMESTALL CT
WILLOWS CT
TUDOR CT
Medical Centre
KEYNES COLLEGE
Playing Field
ROAD
GILES
PARK OAKS
PARK COMMON ROAD
HIGHFIELD CL
Kent College
St Edmunds School
ST THOMAS
NEW
ROAD
OAKS
ROUGH
RAVENSCOURT RD
LOVELL ROAD
Playing Field
UNIVERSITY
NEALS PLACE ROAD
FIRTREE CL
ROSS GDNS
ROSS GARDENS
MAPLE CL
Rough Common
COMMON
CHURCH WOOD CL
STONER COOPER CL
GLEN IRIS AVENUE
GLEN IRIS CL
CHERRY
RICHMOND GDNS
CHERRY GARDEN
CHERRY AV
CHERRY DR
CHERRY DRIVE
CLIF
GARDEN CL
ST MICHAELS CL
MEADOW ROAD
HILLVIEW
HILLSIDE AVENUE
CEDAR VIEW
WESTGA
AVENUE
PALMARS
ROUGH
The Grove
Cemetery
Hall Place

A **B** 34 **C** **D**

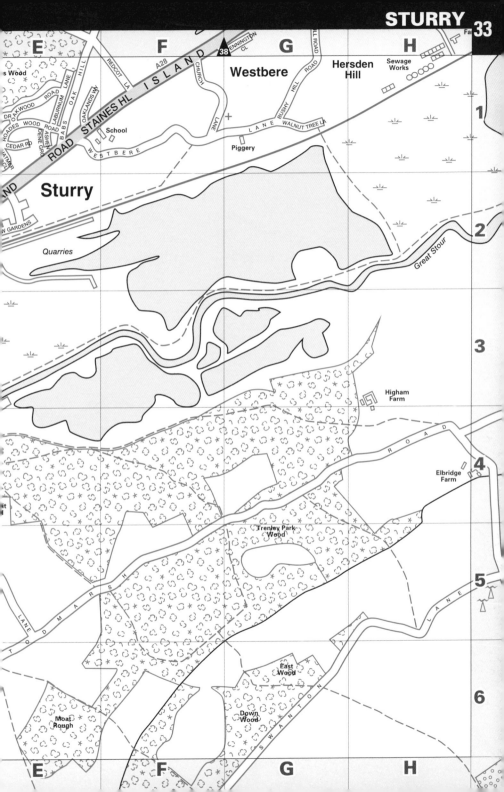

E F 38 G H Fa

Westbere

Hersden Hill

Sewage Works

1

s Wood

OAKWOOD ROAD
DR
HOADES WOOD ROAD
LABURNUM LANE
OAK HILL
REDGOT LA
OAKLANDS W
BABS
CEDAR RD
ASHEN
DENE GRA
HEATHER

A28
STAINES HL
ISLAND
ROAD
CHURCH LANE
PENNINGTON CL

School

LANE

WESTBERE

Piggery

WALNUT TREE LA
BUSHY HILL ROAD
HILL ROAD

Sturry

N GARDENS

Quarries

Great Stour

2

3

Higham Farm

R O A D

Elbridge Farm

4

Trenley Park Wood

5

L A N E

M A R S H

L A N E

East Wood

6

Moat Rough

Down Wood

SWANTON

E F G H

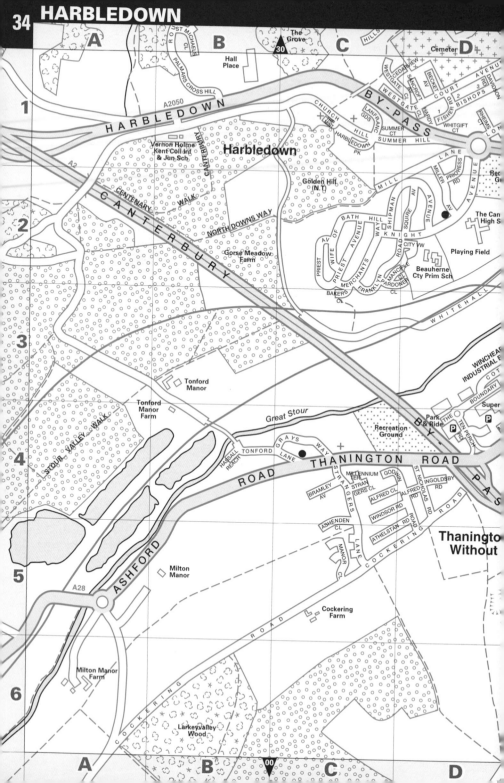

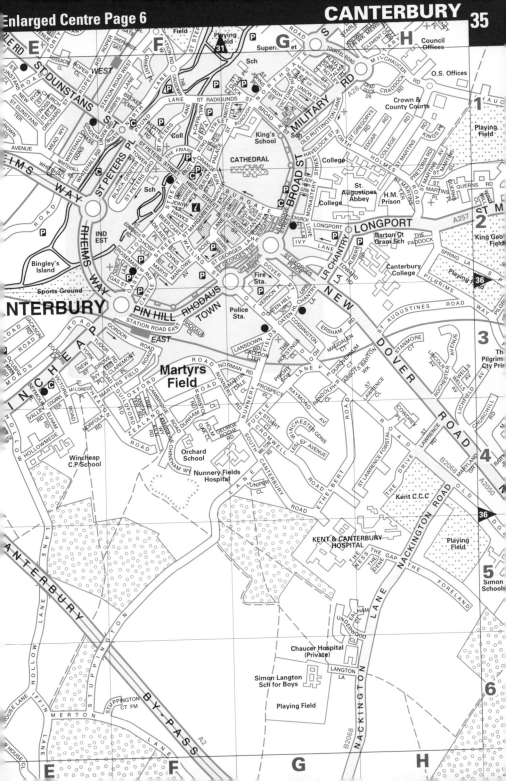

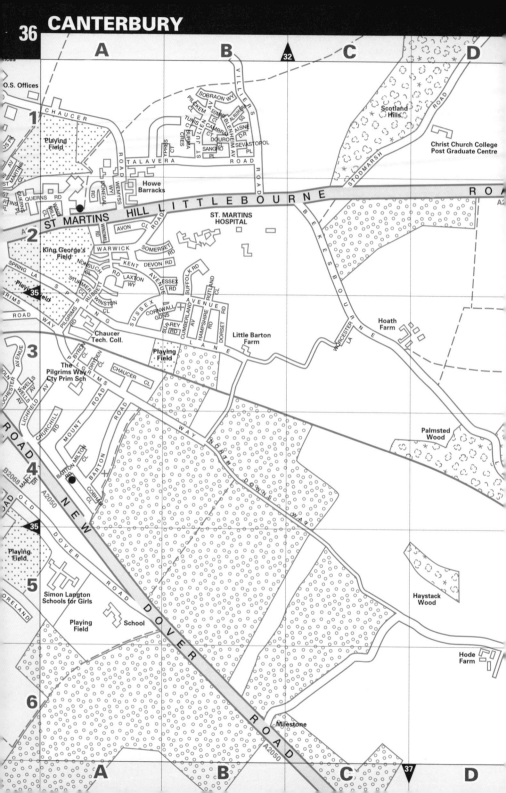

A B 32 C D

O.S. Offices

CHAUCER

Playing
Field

SOBRAON WY
PILKEM
CT
SOMME
BLENHEIM
AV
VILLIERS
AISNE
DR
CAMBRAI
CT
BUILDERS
SQ
TUNIS CI
ST JULIEN
BURMA
CRES
DOURO
CT
SANGRO
PL
SEVASTOPOL
PL

Scotland
Hills

ROAD

Christ Church College
Post Graduate Centre

1

TALAVERA

ROAD
WEMYSS
WY
DONEGAL
RD

Howe
Barracks

ROAD

STODMARSH

QUERNS RD

ST MARTINS HILL LITTLEBOURNE

ROA

A2

ST MARTINS
HOSPITAL

A

AVON CL

WINDMILL

BEKESBOURNE

2

King George's
Field

WARWICK

SOMERSET
RD

SPRING LA

NONSUCH
CL
STURMER
RD
KENT RD
DEVON RD

RUTLAND
CL

RIMS

Playing 35 Field

ROAD

PILGRIMS
WINSTON
CL
LAXTON
WY

ESSEX
RD

SUFFOLK RD

HAMPSHIRE
RD

DORSET RD

Hoath
Farm

WORCESTER LA

SUSSEX

SURREY
RD

CORNWALL
GDNS

CUMBERLAND
AV

AVENUE

WAY

3

AVENUE

Chaucer
Tech. Coll.

BYRON

DRYDEN

PILGRIMS

Playing
Field

CHAUCER
CL

Little Barton
Farm

WELLS AV

LICHFIELD

The
Pilgrims Way
Cty Prim Sch

CHURCHILL
RD

MOUNT

ROAD

LANE

WAY

Palmsted
Wood

4

ROAD

B2068
MARY
CFT

A2050

Barton MILTON
CL

BARTON

COBHAM

NEW

DOWNS

35

DOVER

Playing
Field

MORELAND

5

Simon Langton
Schools for Girls

Playing
Field

School

ROAD

Haystack
Wood

Hode
Farm

6

ROAD

Milestone

A2050

A B C 37 D

A   B   C   D

36

1

2

3

4

5

6

Haystack Wood

Hode Farm

BEKESBOURNE LANE   OAKLEIGH LANE   BEKESBOURNE

BEKESBOURNE LANE

BEKESBOURNE HILL

BEKESBOURNE

ROAD   SCHOOL   LANE

BIFRONS HILL

BIFRONS RD

CRANMER

STATION

Patrixbourne

ST MARYS RD

THE STREET

ROAD

Fords

KEEPERS   HILL

Bifrons Gardens

Bifron's Park

A2

B R I D G E

BEKESBOURNE RD

Elham Valley Way

Nail Bourne

PATRIXBOURNE

Anglo-Saxon Burial Ground

ROAD

HIGH

CONYNGHAM LANE

THE NEW CL

Bridge & Patrixbourne C.E. Prim Sch

Police Office

DERING RD   FILMER RD

THE CLOSE

CHURCHILL CL

UNION

ION PETT HILL

BOURNE VIEW

TER

WESTERN

MILL

Ford

LANE

SAXON GREEN

WINDMILL

BRIDGEFORD WY

BREWERY LA

RIVERSIDE

RIVER SIDE MS

CL

Rec Grd.

PATRIXBOURNE

ROAD

THE STREET

Bridge

B Y

P A S S

Brickfield Farm

Ford

BOURNE PARK ROAD

BOURNE PARK ROAD

B MEADOW CL

BEECH HILL

BRIDGE DOWN

BRIDGE DOWN LA

HIGHAM HILL

PIPPIN AV

Cricket Ground

Higham Park

Cold Stores

Tumuli

Warren Plantation

A2

A   B   C   D

Littlebourne

Ickham

A257 THE HILL HIGH STREET

Reynolds Place
White Bridge
Littlebourne Court
Treasury Farm
Cherry Orchard
Littlebourne C.E. Prim Sch
Rec Grd
Little Stour
Treasury VW

ST VINCENTS CL
THE ELDERS
COURT MEADOWS
PINESIDE RD
HILLCREST RD
EVENHILL RD
NEWING CL
JUBILEE
ROSEACRE RD
ORCHARD CL
THE MALTINGS
THE GREEN
NARGATE
NARGATE CL
ELMLEIGH RD
CHURCH ROAD
HILL ROAD
BUILDERS SQ
COURT
STREET
DRILL
WICKHAM LA
THE STREET
CHERVILLE
SCHOOL
NARGATE STREET
BEKESBOURNE LANE
THE LANE
A257

HERSDEN / WESTBERE

Westbere
Hersden Hill
Hersden

Gravel Pit
Bredlands Farm
Joiners Farm
Hersden Cty Prim Sch
Montgomery School
Playing Field
Haseden Farm
Sewage Works
Hoplands Farm

BREDLANDS ROAD
HOATH ROAD
ROAD ISLAND
A28 ISLAND
PENNINGTON CL
CHURCH LANE
BUSHY HILL ROAD
BUSHY HILL ROAD
THE LANE
WALNUT TREE LA
ST ALBANS RD
SHEFFIELD RD
ASH
THE ELMS
MAPLE CT
MAPLE
OAKS
THE SYCAMORES
SUTTON RD
AVENUE
CRESCENT
THE OAKS
THE POPLARS
EAST VW
NORTH VW
ROAD
EDCO
School
BERE
SHL

Piggery   33

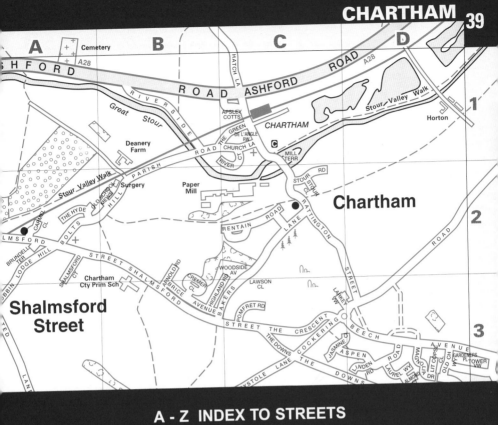

A - Z INDEX TO STREETS
with Postcodes

Orchard,
 stable CT5 — 10 B6
Tree Gdns
2 — 22 B5
le La CT3 — 38 D2
r Rd CT8 — 18 B4
eld Rd CT5 — 10 B5
ut CT2 — 30 A1
ut Dr,
 Ramsgate CT11 — 24 C5
dstairs CT10 — 22 D4
ut Dr,
 terbury CT2 — 33 E1
ut Dr,
 CT14 — 29 F6
ut Dr,
ne Bay CT6 — 11 H4
t Ct CT10 — 5 D1
ster Rd CT12 — 24 C1
m Av CT8 — 17 H3
 Field CT3 — 27 B2
 Gdns CT3 — 27 B2
 La CT11 — 24 B5
 Pl CT3 — 27 B2
 Sq CT3 — 27 B2
am Way CT1 — 35 F4
er Av CT6 — 11 F2
 Av CT11 — 4 A3
 Court Gro
0 — 22 D2
 Fm Way
3 — 28 A4
 Hill,
terbury CT2 — 34 C1
 Hill,
sgate CT11 — 4 C1
 La,
rtham CT4 — 39 C1
 La, Rosemary La,
terbury CT1 — 6 A5
 La,
adigunds,
terbury CT1 — 6 C2
 La,
ry CT2 — 32 C3
 La,
stbere CT2 — 33 F1
 La,
tstable CT5 — 7 A1
 La,
tstable CT5 — 8 B6
 Rd,
adstairs CT10 — 5 C3
 Rd,
terbury CT3 — 38 B2
 Rd,
gate CT9 — 3 E4
 Rd,
sgate CT11 — 4 D1
 Sq CT10 — 5 D3
 St,
adstairs CT10 — 23 E3
 St,
terbury CT1 — 6 D4
 St,
try CT13 — 27 C6
 St,
gate CT9 — 3 E4
 St,
sgate CT12 — 15 B6
 St,
unstans CT2 — 35 E1
 St,
tstable CT5 — 9 G3
 St,
odnesborough
3 — 28 A5
 St*, St Clements,
dwich CT13 — 29 F2
 Street St Marys
3 — 29 E1
 Vw CT6 — 13 F3
 Way CT5 — 10 C3
 Wood Cl CT2 — 30 B6
field Pl CT9 — 3 D3
fields,
adstairs CT10 — 21 E6
fields,
gate CT9 — 3 D4
ill Av CT6 — 13 F2
ill Cl CT4 — 37 A5
ill Rd CT1 — 35 H4
wood Dr CT5 — 10 C5
 Path CT10 — 5 A3
Pl CT10 — 11 F2
w CT2 — 34 D2
t Ct CT10 — 5 C2
am Hill CT5 — 7 D1
Dr CT6 — 11 G4
Rd CT5 — 9 F1

Claremont Gdns CT11 — 24 D3
Claremont Pl CT1 — 6 A6
Claremont St CT6 — 11 H2
Clarence Av CT9 — 20 C3
Clarence Rd,
 Herne Bay CT6 — 12 A2
Clarence Rd,
 Ramsgate CT11 — 24 C5
Clarence St CT6 — 12 B2
Clarendon Gdns CT11 — 4 C2
Clarendon Mews CT10 — 5 A3
Clarendon Rd,
 Broadstairs CT10 — 5 A3
Clarendon Rd,
 Margate CT9 — 19 H2
Clarendon St CT6 — 11 G2
Cleaver La CT11 — 4 D1
Clement Cl CT1 — 31 H6
Clementine Cl CT6 — 13 F2
Clements Rd CT12 — 22 C6
Cliff Av CT6 — 13 F1
Cliff Dr CT6 — 11 H2
Cliff Field CT8 — 17 G2
Cliff Promenade CT10 — 21 H6
Cliff Rd,
 Birchington CT7 — 16 C2
Cliff Rd,
 Broadstairs CT10 — 23 H1
Cliff Rd,
 Whitstable CT5 — 9 G1
Cliff Sea Gro CT6 — 11 H2
Cliff St CT11 — 4 C2
Cliff Ter CT9 — 3 F2
Cliff View Rd CT12 — 26 B5
Cliffe Av CT9 — 18 D3
Clifford Rd CT5 — 9 G4
Cliffsend Gro CT12 — 26 C6
Cliffsend Rd CT12 — 26 C6
Cliffside Dr CT10 — 25 H1
Clifftown Gdns CT6 — 11 G2
Clift Mews CT1 — 19 H1
Clifton Gdns,
 Canterbury CT2 — 30 D6
Clifton Gdns,
 Margate CT9 — 3 F2
Clifton Lawn CT11 — 4 B4
Clifton Pl CT9 — 3 F2
Clifton Rd,
 Margate CT9 — 3 F2
Clifton Rd,
 Ramsgate CT12 — 24 C3
Clifton Rd,
 Whitstable CT5 — 9 E3
Clifton St CT9 — 3 E2
Cliftonville Av,
 Margate CT9 — 20 A3
Cliftonville Av,
 Ramsgate CT12 — 24 C2
Clive Rd,
 Margate CT9 — 22 A3
Clive Rd,
 Ramsgate CT12 — 26 B5
Clovelly Rd CT5 — 9 F5
Clover Rise CT5 — 10 A4
Clowes Ct CT2 — 30 A2
Clyde St CT1 — 35 G1
Coastguard Alley CT5 — 8 D2
Cobbs Pl CT9 — 3 D2
Cobden Pl CT1 — 6 C2
Cobham Cl CT1 — 36 A4
Cockering Rd,
 Canterbury CT1 — 34 A6
Cockering Rd,
 Chartham CT4 — 39 C1
Codrington Rd CT11 — 4 A2
Cogans Ter CT1 — 35 E3
Colburn Rd CT10 — 25 H1
Cold Harbour CT1 — 35 H1
Coleman Cres CT12 — 24 D1
Coleman Stairs CT7 — 17 E2
Colemans Stairs Rd CT7 — 17 E2
Colemans Yard CT11 — 4 C2
Colette Cl CT1 — 21 F3
Colewood Rd CT5 — 10 D3
Collard Cl CT6 — 12 D3
College Rd,
 Canterbury CT1 — 35 H1
College Rd,
 Margate CT9 — 19 F5
College Rd,
 Ramsgate CT11 — 25 E2
College Sq CT9 — 19 G2
Collingwood Cl,
 Broadstairs CT10 — 23 E4

Collingwood Cl,
 Westgate on Sea CT8 — 17 G3
Collingwood Rd CT5 — 9 E3
Collins Rd CT6 — 11 H4
Colombo Sq CT12 — 24 B1
Columbia Av CT5 — 8 C5
Columbine Cl CT5 — 8 D6
Columbus Av CT12 — 15 C2
Conference Walk*,
 Russett Rd CT1 — 36 A2
Conifer Ct*,
 Adrian Sq CT8 — 18 A4
Coniston Av CT11 — 24 B4
Connaught Gdns CT9 — 19 G4
Connaught Rd CT9 — 19 G4
Conrad Av CT1 — 32 A5
Constable Rd CT7 — 16 D2
Consul Cl CT6 — 11 F2
Convent Rd CT10 — 21 E5
Convent Walk CT11 — 24 C5
Conway Cl CT7 — 16 C3
Conyngham Cl CT12 — 24 C1
Conyngham La CT4 — 37 B4
Conyngham Rd,
 Herne Bay CT6 — 13 F1
Conyngham Rd,
 Ramsgate CT12 — 15 B6
Cooks Lea CT13 — 27 B5
Coombe La CT3 — 27 D3
Coombe Walk CT5 — 7 A4
Coopers Hill*,
 Charles La CT1 — 12 C1
Coopers La CT1 — 35 E3
Cop Street Rd CT3 — 27 C1
Copinger Cl CT2 — 31 G4
Copperfield Ct CT10 — 5 D3
Coppergate CT2 — 31 F6
Copperhurst Walk CT9 — 21 E3
Copt Cl CT2 — 32 D1
Cornelis Dr CT12 — 15 B6
Cornford Rd CT7 — 17 E4
Cornhill CT11 — 4 C3
Cornwall Av CT11 — 25 G2
Cornwall Gdns,
 Canterbury CT1 — 36 A3
Cornwall Gdns,
 Margate CT9 — 20 B3
Cornwall Rd CT6 — 11 G4
Cornwallis Av CT6 — 13 E3
Cornwallis Circle CT5 — 9 E3
Cornwallis Gdns CT10 — 23 G2
Coronation Cl CT10 — 21 E6
Coronation Cres CT9 — 19 G4
Coronation Rd CT11 — 4 A2
Corsican Walk*,
 Cornwallis Walk CT6 — 13 F3
Corylus Dr CT5 — 8 C5
Cossington Rd CT1 — 6 D5
Cottage Rd CT11 — 4 D2
Cottage Row CT13 — 29 E1
Cottington Rd CT12 — 26 A6
Cotton Rd CT1 — 34 D3
Coulter Rd CT6 — 11 G4
Court Hill CT3 — 38 A1
Court Mdws CT3 — 38 A2
Court Rd CT7 — 14 A5
Courtlands CT6 — 12 D3
Courtlands Cl CT12 — 26 C6
Courtlands Way CT8 — 18 A3
Coventry Gdns CT6 — 13 G1
Cow La CT1 — 34 D3
Cowdrey Pl CT1 — 35 H4
Cowley Rise CT9 — 20 B6
Cowper Cl CT5 — 10 C3
Cowper Rd CT9 — 3 E4
Coxes Av CT12 — 22 B5
Coxes La CT12 — 22 B5
Craddock Dr CT1 — 35 H1
Craddock Rd CT1 — 35 H1
Crampton Ct CT10 — 5 A3
Cranbourne Cl CT11 — 25 G2
Cranbourne Walk CT2 — 31 E5
Cranbrook Cl CT9 — 21 E4
Cranleigh Gdns CT5 — 9 F4
Cranmer Cl CT4 — 37 C2
Craven Cl CT9 — 18 D5
Crawford Gdns CT9 — 20 A3
Crawford Rd CT10 — 23 F3
Cremer Cl CT4 — 39 B2
Crescent Rd,
 Birchington CT7 — 17 E3
Crescent Rd,
 Broadstairs CT10 — 21 G5

Crescent Rd,
 Margate CT9 — 3 A3
Crescent Rd,
 Ramsgate CT11 — 24 D4
Cresta Cl CT6 — 11 E2
Crispe Rd CT7 — 16 C6
Crofton Rd CT8 — 18 A5
Crofts Pl CT10 — 5 C3
Cromwell Rd,
 Canterbury CT1 — 35 G4
Cromwell Rd,
 Whitstable CT5 — 9 E3
Cross Rd CT7 — 17 E3
Cross St,
 Canterbury CT2 — 35 E1
Cross St,
 Herne Bay CT6 — 12 A3
Crossley Av CT6 — 11 E2
Crossways CT2 — 31 F4
Crossways Av CT9 — 22 A3
Crow Hill CT10 — 5 B1
Crow Hill Rd CT9 — 18 C5
Crown Gdns CT2 — 35 E1
Crown Hill Rd CT6 — 11 G2
Crundale Way CT9 — 21 E4
Cudham Gdns CT9 — 20 D3
Culpepper CT2 — 31 G4
Cumberland Av,
 Broadstairs CT10 — 5 B1
Cumberland Av,
 Canterbury CT1 — 36 B3
Cumberland Rd,
 Margate CT9 — 20 A3
Cumberland Rd,
 Ramsgate CT11 — 4 A2
Cundishall Cl CT5 — 8 D4
Cunningham Cres CT7 — 16 C3
Curlew Cl CT6 — 13 E4
Curlinge Ct CT11 — 24 B5
Curtis Wood Park Rd CT6 — 14 C2
Curtis Wood Rd CT6 — 14 C2
Cushman Rd CT1 — 35 E3
Cuthbert Rd CT8 — 17 H2
Cypress Cl CT5 — 8 D5

Daimler Av CT6 — 11 F2
Dalby Rd CT9 — 3 F2
Dalby Sq CT9 — 3 F2
Dallinger Rd CT7 — 16 D2
Dalmaney Cl CT10 — 5 C2
Dalmeny Av CT10 — 20 C4
Damerham Cl CT2 — 31 E5
Dane Court Gdns CT10 — 22 D2
Dane Court Rd CT10 — 22 C1
Dane Cres CT11 — 25 F2
Dane End Rd CT8 — 17 H2
Dane Gdns CT9 — 20 B6
Dane Hill CT9 — 3 E2
Dane Hill Gro CT9 — 3 E2
Dane Hill Row CT9 — 3 E2
Dane Mount CT9 — 20 B6
Dane Park Rd,
 Margate CT9 — 3 F3
Dane Park Rd,
 Ramsgate CT11 — 25 F2
Dane Rd,
 Birchington CT7 — 16 A3
Dane Rd, Margate CT9 — 3 E2
Dane Rd,
 Ramsgate CT11 — 25 F3
Dane Valley Rd CT9 — 20 A5
Danesmead Ter CT9 — 3 F3
Daniels Ct CT5 — 8 D3
Darenth Cl CT6 — 12 D4
Dargate Rd CT5 — 7 A4
Darnley Cl CT10 — 23 F5
Darrell Cl CT6 — 11 H3
Darren Gdns CT10 — 25 G1
Darwin Rd,
 Birchington CT7 — 16 D3
Darwin Rd,
 Canterbury CT2 — 31 E3
Daryngton Av CT7 — 16 A3
David Av CT9 — 20 C3
Davids Cl CT10 — 5 C5
Davidson Rd CT2 — 34 D1
Daytona Way CT6 — 11 E2
De L'Angle Row CT4 — 39 C1
Deal Rd CT13 — 29 E5
Dean Cft CT6 — 13 E5
Deane Cl CT5 — 9 F5
Deansway Av CT2 — 32 C1
Deborah Cl CT5 — 9 G5
Delacourt Cl CT12 — 26 B2
Delaware Cl CT2 — 32 D2
Delf St CT13 — 29 E1

Delfside CT13 — 29 F3
Delmar Cl CT5 — 10 C3
Denbigh Rd CT12 — 24 B2
Dence Cl CT6 — 12 D2
Dence Pk CT6 — 12 D2
Dene Walk CT9 — 19 G5
Denmark Rd CT11 — 25 F3
Denne Cl CT2 — 32 D1
Denstead Ct CT2 — 30 C4
Dent-de-Lion Ct CT9 — 18 B5
Dent-de-Lion Rd,
 Margate CT9 — 18 C5
Dent-de-Lion Rd,
 Westgate on Sea CT8 — 17 H2
Denton Way CT9 — 20 B4
Dering Cl CT4 — 37 B4
Dering Rd,
 Canterbury CT4 — 37 B4
Dering Rd,
 Herne Bay CT6 — 12 B2
Derwent Av CT11 — 24 B4
D'Este Rd CT11 — 4 F1
Detling Av CT10 — 25 G1
Devon Ct*,
 Stirling Way CT12 — 24 C1
Devon Gdns CT7 — 16 D4
Devon Rd CT1 — 36 A2
Devonshire Gdns CT9 — 20 B3
Devonshire Ter CT10 — 5 C3
Diamond Rd CT5 — 9 F2
Dickens Av CT1 — 32 A6
Dickens Rd CT10 — 5 C2
Dickens Walk CT10 — 5 C3
Discovery Walk*,
 Russett Rd CT1 — 36 A2
Doggerel Acre CT5 — 9 G5
Dolphin Cl CT10 — 21 F3
Dolphin St CT6 — 12 B1
Domneva Rd,
 Ramsgate CT12 — 15 B5
Domneva Rd,
 Westgate on Sea CT8 — 17 H2
Donegal Rd CT1 — 36 A2
Donnahay Rd CT12 — 22 C5
Dorcas Gdns CT10 — 23 G2
Doric Cl CT11 — 24 D5
Dorothy Dr CT12 — 22 C6
Dorset Cl CT5 — 8 C5
Dorset Gdns CT7 — 16 D4
Dorset Rd CT1 — 36 B3
Douglas Av CT5 — 9 F3
Douglas Cl CT10 — 23 E3
Douglas Rd CT6 — 12 C3
Douro Cl CT1 — 36 B1
Dove Cl CT5 — 8 D5
Dovedale Ct CT7 — 17 F4
Dover Rd CT13 — 28 D5
Dover St CT11 — 6 D4
Down Barton Rd CT7 — 14 A6
Downs Av CT5 — 9 F3
Downs Pk CT6 — 12 D2
Downs Rd,
 Canterbury CT2 — 31 F4
Downs Rd,
 Ramsgate CT11 — 24 B5
Drainless Rd CT8 — 28 A6
Drapers Av CT9 — 19 G4
Drapers Cl CT9 — 19 H5
Drill La CT3 — 38 C1
Drybeck Av CT11 — 24 A3
Dryden Cl CT1 — 36 A3
Duck La CT1 — 6 C2
Dudley Av CT8 — 17 G2
Duke St CT9 — 3 D2
Dumpton Gap Rd CT10 — 23 G6
Dumpton La CT11 — 25 F2
Dumpton Park Dr CT11 — 25 G3
Dumpton Park Rd CT11 — 25 F2
Duncan Cl CT5 — 9 E5
Duncan Dr CT7 — 16 C3
Duncan Rd,
 Ramsgate CT11 — 4 A2
Duncan Rd,
 Whitstable CT5 — 9 E4
Dundonald Rd,
 Broadstairs CT10 — 5 C4
Dundonald Rd,
 Ramsgate CT11 — 24 D4
Dunedin Rd CT12 — 24 B1
Dunoon Ct*,
 Argyll Dr CT11 — 25 G1
Dunstan Av CT8 — 17 G4
Durban Cl CT12 — 24 B1

Dene CT10 23 E3
...ells Rd CT6 11 G2
...wn Rd CT9 19 E3
...erry Vw CT5 8 D6
...Ct CT6 13 F5
...Dr CT5 10 A5
... St CT5 9 E4
... Reach CT1 34 B4
...s Av CT9 19 H3
...s Pl CT13 29 E3
...a CT4 39 C1
... Rd,
...ate CT9 3 A3
... Rd,
...sgate CT11 4 A1
...ck Pl CT3 27 C2
...ck St CT1 6 D3
...Dr CT6 13 H1
...Cl CT2 31 G4
...arm Way CT6 12 D5
...Cl CT2 24 C4
...Cl CT5 8 D5
...urst Cl CT7 17 E2
...urst Way
23 G6
...La CT1 6 B4
...Rd CT6 11 G4
... Sq CT9 3 D3
... St CT9 3 D2
...orn Av CT2 31 G5
...orn Cl CT11 25 E1
...ll CT13 27 D6
...here Dr CT6 13 F1
...ood Mdw
3 29 E3
...here Rd CT5 8 B5
...orn Dr CT2 31 G3
...orn Gdns CT9 20 D3
...n Hand Rd
13 H5
...Cl CT2 32 C1
...er Cl CT9 19 E4
...wood Dr CT1 25 F1
...n Rd CT1 35 E3
...g Cl CT6 13 E4
...a Av CT9 19 G4
...ion Cl CT12 22 C6
...lyn Av CT1 24 C3
...st Av CT9 20 A4
...st Rd,
...hington CT7 16 B3
...st Rd,
...stgate on Sea
17 G2
...Ct CT1 6 B6
...rt Rd CT11 24 D4
...ord Gdns CT7 16 D4
...on Rd CT11 25 F3
...ward Av CT7 16 C2
...ge Cl CT5 8 B6
... Av CT6 12 D3
... Bay Rd,
...nterbury CT2 32 C1
... Bay Rd,
...itstable CT5 10 A3
...a Dr CT6 11 H3
...e St CT6 12 C6
...ville Gdns CT6 12 D3
...den Rd CT13 27 A6
...hell Rd CT7 16 D2
...ord Pl CT11 4 C3
...ord Rd CT9 20 B5
...ord St CT11 4 C3
...r Pl CT12 31 G5
...nia St CT11 4 D2
...St, Bridge CT4 37 A4
...oadstairs CT10 5 A3
...St,
...nterbury CT1
...St, Eastry CT13 27 B5
...St,
...rdwich CT2 32 D4
...St, Garlinge CT9 18 C5
...St,
...rne Bay CT6 12 B2
...St,
...ttlebourne CT3 38 A2
...St,
...anston CT12 26 D3
...St, Margate CT9 3 C2
...St,
...inster CT12 15 B5
...St,
...orthgate CT1 6 D2
...St,
...amsgate CT11 4 C1
...St,
...andwich CT13 29 F2

High St,
St Lawrence CT11 24 C4
High St,
St Peters CT10 23 E3
High St, Sturry CT2 32 D3
High St,
Whitstable CT5 9 E2
High View Av CT6 11 G1
Higham La CT4 37 C6
Highbury Gdns CT12 22 B5
Highfield Cl,
Canterbury CT2 30 C5
Highfield Cl,
Ramsgate CT12 22 B5
Highfield Gdns CT9 3 A4
Highfield Rd CT12 22 B5
Highfields Av CT6 13 F2
Highfields Vw CT6 13 F2
Highgate Rd,
Whitstable CT5 10 A5
Highland Rd,
Canterbury CT4 39 B3
Hilary Cl CT6 13 F2
Hildersham Cl CT10 23 E2
Hill Dr CT13 27 C5
Hill House Dr CT12 15 B4
Hill Top Rd CT6 12 D2
Hillborough Dr CT6 13 H1
Hillborough Pk CT6 13 H2
Hillborough Rd CT6 13 E2
Hillbrow Av,
Canterbury CT2 32 D1
Hillbrow Av,
Herne Bay CT6 12 D4
Hillbrow Rd CT11 25 E2
Hillcrest Gdns CT11 24 C4
Hillcrest Rd CT3 38 A2
Hillcroft Rd CT6 12 D4
Hiller Cl CT10 23 F2
Hillman Av CT6 11 F2
Hills Court Rd CT3 27 D2
Hills Cl CT3 27 D1
Hillside Av CT2 30 C6
Hillside Rd CT5 9 H3
Hillview Rd,
Canterbury CT2 30 C6
Hillview Rd,
Whitstable CT5 9 E4
Hinchliffe Way CT9 20 C5
Hoades Wood Rd
CT2 33 E1
Hoath Rd CT3 38 A4
Hobart Rd CT12 24 B1
Hockeredge Gdns
CT9 18 B4
Hodges Gap CT9 20 B2
Hodgson Rd CT5 8 A5
Hogarth Cl CT6 13 G2
Hogs Corner CT13 14 D1
Holborn Cl CT6 14 D1
Holbrook Dr CT12 24 C1
Holiday Sq CT9 3 D2
Holland Cl CT10 21 G4
Hollicondane Rd
CT11 25 E3
Hollow La CT1 35 E4
Hollowmede CT1 35 E4
Holly Cl CT10 22 C4
Holly Gdns CT9 20 C4
Holly La CT9 20 B3
Holly Rd CT11 25 F2
Holm Oak Cl CT1 35 F4
Holm Oak Gdns CT10 23 F4
Holmscroft Rd CT6 13 F2
Holness Rd CT3 27 B1
Holton Cl CT7 17 E5
Holy Ghost Alley*,
St Peters St CT13 29 F2
Homefern Ho CT9 3 D2
Homeleigh Rd CT12 22 B5
Homestall Ct CT2 30 C4
Homestead Village
CT11 24 D5
Homewood Rd CT12 32 D2
Honeysuckle Cl CT9 19 E5
Honeysuckle Rd CT11 25 G3
Honeysuckle Way
CT6 13 F4
Honeywood Cl CT1 31 H6
Honfleur Rd CT13 29 E2
Hoopers La CT6 13 F4
Hopes La CT12 22 C5
Hopeville Av CT10 22 D2
Hornet Cl CT10 22 D4
Horsa Rd CT7 16 B3
Horsebridge Rd CT5 9 E2
Hoser Gdns CT7 17 E3
Hospital La CT1 6 B4
Hovenden Cl CT2 31 G4

Howard Rd CT10 5 A5
Hubert Way CT10 23 E2
Hudson Cl CT2 32 D2
Hudson Rd CT1 31 H6
Hugin Av CT10 20 D6
Humber Av CT6 11 E2
Hundreds Cl CT8 17 H3
Hunters Chase,
Herne Bay CT6 13 F5
Hunters Chase,
Whitstable CT5 9 F5
Hunters Forstal Rd
CT6 13 E5
Hunting Gate CT7 16 D3
Hunton Gdns CT2 31 G3
Hurst Gro CT12 24 D1
Hythe Pl CT13 29 F3

Iffin La CT1 35 E6
Ince Rd CT1 32 D1

INDUSTRIAL & RETAIL:

All Saints Ind Est
CT9 3 B4
Broadlands Ind Est
CT2 30 A1
Canterbury Retail Pk
CT1 32 B4
City Bsns Pk CT1 32 A5
Crystal Bsns Centre
CT13 29 G1
East Kent Retail Pk
CT10 22 B3
Eddington Bsns Pk
CT6 12 B4
Goodwyn Pk CT9 22 A3
Haine Ind Est CT12 24 A2
John Wilson Bsns Pk
CT5 10 A4
Joseph Wilson Ind Est
CT5 9 H5
Manston Pk CT12 15 C1
Pysons Rd Ind Est
CT10 22 C5
St Augustines Bsns Pk
CT5 10 D3
Sandwich Ind Est
CT13 29 G1
Telegraph Hill Ind Est
CT12 15 C4
The Centre CT9 3 D3
Westwood Ind Est
CT9 19 H6
Westwood Retail Pk
CT9 22 A3
Whitefriars Shopping
Centre CT1 6 C4
Wincheap Ind Est
CT1 34 D3

Ingle Cl CT7 17 F3
Ingoldsby Rd,
Birchington CT7 16 B3
Ingoldsby Rd,
Canterbury CT1 34 D4
Inverness Ter CT10 5 B4
Invicta Rd,
Margate CT9 20 B5
Invicta Rd,
Whitstable CT5 9 G3
Irchester St CT11 4 E1
Iron Bar La CT1 6 C4
Irvine Dr CT9 20 C5
Island Rd,
Hersden CT3 38 A6
Island Rd,
Sturry CT2 32 D2
Island Wall CT5 8 D3
Ivanhoe Cl,
Herne Bay CT6 12 D3
Ivanhoe Rd,
Westgate on Sea
CT8 18 A4
Ivy House Rd CT5 9 G3
Ivy La,
Canterbury CT1 6 D4
Ivy La, Ramsgate CT11 4 B3
Ivy Pl CT1 6 D4
Ivychurch Gdns CT9 21 E3

Jackson Rd CT1 35 E3
Jacob Cl CT9 19 F5
James Cl CT3 27 B2
James St CT11 4 E1
Jasmine Cl CT4 39 C3
Jayne Walk CT5 8 C6
Jennifer Gdns CT7 20 C6
Jessica Mews*,
Military Rd CT1 31 H6

Jesuit Cl CT2 31 G4
Jewry La CT1 6 B3
John St CT10 5 C4
Johns Grn CT13 28 D4
Joseph Conrad Ho*,
Bishops Way CT2 34 D1
Joss Gap Rd CT10 21 G4
Joy La CT5 8 B5
Jubilee Cl CT10 5 C4
Jubilee Rd,
Canterbury CT3 38 A2
Jubilee Rd,
Sandwich CT13 29 E2
Jubilee Rd,
Worth CT14 29 G6
Julie Cl CT10 23 F1
Junction Rd CT6 11 G4
Juniper Cl,
Canterbury CT1 35 G4
Juniper Cl,
Whitstable CT5 9 G3

Keat Farm Cl CT6 13 H2
Keepers Hill CT4 37 D3
Keith Av CT12 24 B2
Kemp Rd CT5 10 B4
Kemsing Gdns CT2 31 H4
Kendal Cl CT11 24 C4
Kendal Rise CT10 5 A1
Kennedy Ho CT11 4 E2
Kensington Rd CT1 32 A4
Kent Av CT1 16 D3
Kent Gdns CT7 4 E2
Kent Pl CT11 20 B5
Kent Rd CT9 9 E4
Kent St CT5 9 E4
Kent Ter CT11 4 E2
Kentmere Av CT11 24 A4
Kenton Gdns CT13 24 B5
Kevin Dr CT11 24 C5
Keyworth Mews CT1 31 H6
Kilbride Cl*,
Argyll Dr CT11 25 G1
Kilndown Gdns,
Canterbury CT2 31 G4
Kilndown Gdns,
Margate CT9 20 D3
Kimberley Gro CT5 8 B6
Kimberley Rd CT12 24 B1
King Arthur Rd CT12 26 C4
King Edward Av,
Broadstairs CT10 5 B4
King Edward Av,
Herne Bay CT6 13 E2
King Edward Rd,
Birchington CT7 16 D5
King Edward Rd,
Ramsgate CT11 24 D4
King Edward St CT5 9 E3
King St,
Canterbury CT1 6 C3
King St,
Fordwich CT2 32 D4
King St, Margate CT9 3 D2
King St,
Ramsgate CT11 4 D2
King St,
Sandwich CT13 29 F2
Kingfisher Cl,
Margate CT9 18 C5
Kingfisher Cl,
Whitstable CT5 8 D5
Kingfisher Ct CT6 12 A4
Kingfisher Walk
CT10 23 E3
Kings Av,
Birchington CT7 16 B3
Kings Av,
Broadstairs CT10 5 B1
Kings Av,
Ramsgate CT12 24 C2
Kings Av,
Whitstable CT5 9 G3
Kings Pk CT1 35 H1
Kings Pl CT11 4 D2
Kings Rd,
Birchington CT7 17 E5
Kings Rd,
Herne Bay CT6 12 B2
Kings Rd,
Ramsgate CT11 25 E3
Kingsdown Pk CT5 9 G1
Kingsfield Rd CT6 13 E4
Kingsgate Av CT10 21 E4
Kingsgate Bay Rd
CT10 21 G3
Kingsley Rd CT5 9 F4
Kingsmead Rd CT1 6 D1
Kingston Av CT9 18 D5

Kingston Cl,
Herne Bay CT6 13 H2
Kingston Cl,
Ramsgate CT12 24 C1
Kirbys La CT2 6 A2
Kirkstone Av CT11 24 A4
Kite Fm CT5 10 C2
Knight Av CT2 34 C2
Knightrider St CT13 29 F2
Knights Av CT10 5 C1
Knockholt Rd CT9 21 E2
Knold Pk CT9 19 F5
Knotts La CT1 6 C2
Knowler Way CT6 13 F2
Knowlton Walk CT1 31 H6

La Belle Alliance Sq
CT11 4 E1
Laburnum Av CT13 29 E3
Laburnum La CT2 33 E1
Lady Woottons Grn
CT1 6 D3
Ladyfields CT6 13 F5
Ladysmith Gro CT5 8 B6
Ladysmith Rd CT5 7 C2
Lagos Av CT12 24 B2
Laking Av CT10 23 G1
Laleham Gdns CT9 20 B4
Laleham Rd CT9 20 B4
Laleham Walk CT9 20 A5
Lamberhurst Way
CT9 21 E3
Lambeth Rd CT1 32 A4
Lambourne Walk*,
Russett Rd CT1 36 A2
Lambs Walk CT5 8 D6
Laming Rd CT7 17 E4
Lancaster Cl CT12 24 C1
Lancaster Gdns,
Birchington CT7 16 D4
Lancaster Gdns,
Herne Bay CT6 13 G1
Lancaster Rd CT1 35 F3
Lanchester Cl CT6 11 F3
Landon Rd CT6 13 E2
Lane End CT6 12 A2
Lanfranc Gdns CT2 34 C1
Lang Ct CT5 10 B3
Langdale Av CT1 24 B4
Langdon Av CT3 27 D3
Langham Cl CT9 18 C4
Langley Gdns CT9 20 D2
Langton La CT1 35 G6
Lansdown Rd CT1 6 C6
Lanthorne Rd CT10 23 F1
Larch Cl CT10 22 D4
Larkey Vw CT4 39 C3
Latimer Cl CT6 11 F3
Laundry Rd CT12 15 C5
Laureate Cl CT9 20 B4
Laurel Way CT4 39 D3
Laurensfield CT12 15 B4
Lauriston Cl CT11 24 B5
Lauriston Mount CT10 5 A1
Lausanne Rd CT9 3 E3
Lavender Cl,
Margate CT9 19 E4
Lavender Cl,
Whitstable CT5 10 B4
Lawley Cl CT12 24 D1
Lawn Rd CT10 5 A3
Lawn Villas CT11 4 C2
Lawrence Gdns CT6 13 E3
Lawson Cl CT4 39 C3
Laxton Way,
Canterbury CT1 36 A2
Laxton Way,
Whitstable CT5 10 B5
Lay La CT3 27 C2
Laylam Cl CT10 22 D3
Leas Grn CT10 22 D4
Leatt Cl CT10 23 E4
Leggetts La*,
Sea St CT5 9 E2
Leicester Av CT9 20 C3
Leigh Rd CT12 24 A2
Leighville Dr CT6 12 A3
Lenham Cl CT10 23 F6
Lenham Gdns CT9 18 C5
Leonards Av CT11 25 F2
Leopold Rd CT11 25 F2
Leopold St CT11 4 D2
Lerryn Gdns CT11 21 E5
Lesley Av CT11 35 G4
Leslie Av CT9 18 C5
Leslie Rd CT7 17 E2
Lewis Cres CT9 20 A2
Leybourn Rd CT10 5 C6
Leybourne Dr CT9 18 C5

Orchard St CT2 35 E1
Orchard Vw CT3 27 D3
Orient Pl CT2 6 B1
Osborne Gdns CT6 13 F2
Osborne Rd CT10 23 F4
Osborne Ter CT9 3 E4
Osbourn Av CT8 17 H2
Osbourne Rd CT10 5 A4
Oscar Rd CT10 5 C4
Osprey Cl CT5 8 D5
Otham Cl CT2 31 G4
Owls Hatch Rd CT6 11 G5
Oxenden Park Dr CT6 12 A3
Oxenden Sq CT6 12 A2
Oxenden St CT6 12 A2
Oxford Rd CT1 35 F3
Oxford St, Margate CT9 3 E4
Oxford St, Whitstable CT5 9 E3
Oxney Cl CT7 16 D3
Oyster Cl CT1 11 G3

Packers La CT11 4 D1
Paddock Rd CT7 17 E4
Paddock Vw CT5 9 F5
Paffard Ct CT2 32 D1
Pafford Ct CT2 32 D1
Palace Cl CT5 10 A4
Palace St CT1 6 C3
Palm Bay Av CT9 20 B2
Palm Bay Gdns CT9 20 B2
Palmars Cross Hill CT2 34 B1
Palmer Cl CT6 12 D6
Palmer Cres CT9 20 B5
Palmerston Av CT10 5 C5
Paradise CT11 4 B1
Paradise Row CT13 29 E1
Paragon Royal Par CT11 4 C4
Paragon St CT11 4 C4
Pardoner Cl CT2 34 C2
Parham Cl CT1 31 H6
Parham Rd CT1 31 H5
Parish Rd CT4 39 B2
Park Av, Birchington CT7 16 D4
Park Av, Broadstairs CT10 23 E6
Park Av, Whitstable CT5 9 G1
Park Chase CT10 23 E6
Park Crescent CT9 3 E3
Park Farm Cl CT2 31 E2
Park Gate CT10 23 E6
Park La, Birchington CT7 17 E4
Park La, Margate CT9 3 F3
Park Pl, Herne Bay CT6 14 D1
Park Pl, Margate CT9 3 D3
Park Rd, Birchington CT7 17 E4
Park Rd, Broadstairs CT10 23 H2
Park Rd, Herne Bay CT6 12 B2
Park Rd, Margate CT9 3 F3
Park Rd, Ramsgate CT11 25 E3
Park Vw CT2 32 D1
Park Wood Cl CT10 25 F1
Park Wood Rd CT2 30 C3
Parkland Ct CT10 23 F2
Parkwood Cl CT10 23 E6
Parsonage Rd CT6 12 C4
Patricia Way CT10 22 C5
Patrixbourne Rd CT4 37 B5
Payton Cl CT9 19 H6
Payton Mews*, Military Rd CT1 31 H6
Peak Dr CT13 27 B5
Pean Court Rd CT5 7 D3
Pean Hill CT5 7 E3
Pear Tree Cl CT10 22 C4
Pearmain Walk*, Russett Rd CT1 36 A2
Pearsons Way CT10 20 D6
Peartree Rd CT6 13 E4
Peelers Ct CT2 6 B1
Pegwell Av CT11 24 C6
Pegwell Cl CT11 24 B5
Pegwell Rd CT11 24 B6
Pembroke Av CT5 18 C3
Pengelly Pl CT2 31 F6
Pennington Cl CT3 38 A6
Penshurst Cl CT2 31 G5

Penshurst Gdns CT9 21 E3
Penshurst Rd CT11 25 G3
Percy Av CT10 21 E4
Percy Rd, Broadstairs CT10 5 A2
Percy Rd, Margate CT9 19 H1
Percy Rd, Ramsgate CT11 25 E3
Perkins Av CT9 19 G4
Petchell Mews*, Military Rd CT1 31 H6
Pett Hill CT4 37 A4
Pettman Cl CT6 12 C3
Petts Cres CT12 15 B6
Philip Corby Cl CT9 20 B3
Phillips Rd CT7 17 E4
Picton Rd CT11 24 D4
Pier App CT10 5 D3
Pier Av, Herne Bay CT6 12 A3
Pier Av, Whitstable CT5 9 H1
Pier Chine CT6 12 B2
Pier Yd CT11 4 E2
Pierpoint Rd CT5 9 E5
Pierremont Av CT10 5 B3
Pigeon La CT6 12 D4
Pilckem Cl CT1 36 B1
Pilgrims La CT5 7 B2
Pilgrims Rd CT1 36 A3
Pilgrims Way CT1 35 H2
Pin Hill CT1 6 A5
Pine Tree Av CT2 31 E6
Pine Walk CT6 13 H1
Pineside Rd CT3 38 A1
Pinetree Cl, Birchington CT7 17 E3
Pinetree Cl, Whitstable CT5 9 G1
Pinewood Cl CT12 24 D2
Pintail Way CT6 13 E4
Pippin Av CT4 37 C6
Plains of Waterloo CT11 4 E1
Plantation Rd CT5 10 C4
Plenty Brook Dr CT6 12 B4
Pleydell Cres CT2 32 D1
Plough Cl CT6 13 F4
Plough La CT5 10 C2
Pluckley Gdns CT9 20 D3
Plumpton Walk*, Military Rd CT1 31 H6
Plumstone Rd CT12 15 A1
Poets Corner CT9 19 H3
Pollard Pl CT5 8 D6
Polo Way CT5 10 C5
Pomfret Rd CT4 39 C3
Poorhole La CT10 22 A3
Popes La CT2 32 C1
Poplar Dr CT6 11 H3
Poplar Rd, Broadstairs CT10 23 E2
Poplar Rd, Ramsgate CT11 4 B1
Potten Street Rd CT7 14 A4
Potter St CT13 29 F1
Poulders Gdns CT13 28 D3
Poulders Rd CT13 28 C2
Poulton La CT3 27 A3
Pound La CT1 6 B2
Powell Cotton Dr CT7 17 E4
Prestedge Av CT11 23 E6
Preston Par CT5 8 A5
Preston Rd CT12 26 D2
Pretoria Rd CT1 35 H2
Prices Av, Margate CT9 20 A3
Prices Av, Ramsgate CT11 24 D4
Priest Av CT2 34 C2
Priest Fields CT6 13 H1
Priest Walk CT5 10 A3
Primrose Way, Ramsgate CT12 26 B6
Primrose Way, Whitstable CT5 10 B5
Prince Andrew Rd CT10 21 E6
Prince Charles Rd CT10 20 D6
Prince Edwards Promenade CT11 24 C6
Princes Av CT12 24 C2
Princes Cl CT7 16 B3
Princes Cres CT9 3 E3
Princes Gdns CT9 20 B3
Princes Rd CT11 25 E2
Princes St,

Margate CT9 3 D3
Princes St, Ramsgate CT11 4 C2
Princes Walk CT9 20 D2
Princes Way CT2 35 E1
Princess Anne Rd CT10 20 D6
Princess Cl CT5 10 B3
Princess Margaret Av, Margate CT9 20 D3
Princess Margaret Av, Ramsgate CT12 24 B1
Princess Rd CT5 10 B3
Prioress Rd CT12 34 D2
Priory Cl CT10 23 F5
Priory Gdns CT1 6 D6
Priory La CT6 12 C4
Priory of St Jacob CT1 35 E4
Priory Rd CT11 4 B3
Promenade, Broadstairs CT10 5 C4
Promenade, Margate CT9 3 E1
Prospect Cl CT8 18 A5
Prospect Gdns CT12 15 A5
Prospect Hill CT6 12 C1
Prospect Pl, Broadstairs CT10 5 C3
Prospect Pl, Canterbury CT1 35 G3
Prospect Rd, Birchington CT7 16 D3
Prospect Rd, Broadstairs CT10 5 C3
Prospect Rd, Ramsgate CT12 15 A5
Prospect Ter CT11 4 C3
Puckle La CT1 6 D6
Pudding La CT3 27 B2
Pullman Cl CT12 24 D2
Pump La CT9 3 D3
Purchas Ct CT2 30 C3
Pye Alley La CT5 7 C3
Pyott Mews*, Military Rd CT1 31 H6
Pysons Rd CT12 22 C6

Quantock Gdns CT12 22 B5
Quay La CT13 29 F2
Queen Bertha Rd CT11 24 D5
Queen Berthas Av CT7 17 G3
Queen Elizabeth Av CT9 20 C4
Queen St, Herne Bay CT6 12 B2
Queen St, Ramsgate CT11 4 C2
Queens Av, Birchington CT7 16 B3
Queens Av, Broadstairs CT10 5 C1
Queens Av, Canterbury CT2 34 D1
Queens Av, Herne Bay CT6 13 F2
Queens Av, Margate CT9 3 D4
Queens Av, Ramsgate CT12 24 C2
Queens Gate Rd CT11 24 D3
Queens Gdns, Broadstairs CT10 5 C5
Queens Gdns, Herne Bay CT6 12 C2
Queens Gdns, Margate CT9 19 H1
Queens Promenade CT9 20 A2
Queens Rd, Broadstairs CT10 5 B4
Queens Rd, Canterbury CT3 27 C1
Queens Rd, Ramsgate CT11 25 G3
Queens Rd, Westgate on Sea CT8 18 B4
Queens Rd, Whitstable CT5 9 G2
Queensbridge Dr CT6 11 H1
Querns Pl CT1 35 H2
Querns Rd CT1 35 H2
Quetta Rd CT12 24 B1
Quex Cl CT8 18 B5
Quex View Rd CT7 16 D5

Margate CT9 3 D3
Princes St,
Ramsgate CT11 4 C2
Princes Walk CT9 20 D2
Princes Way CT2 35 E1
Princess Anne Rd CT10 20 D6
Princess Cl CT5 10 B3
Princess Margaret Av, Margate CT9 20 D3
Princess Margaret Av, Ramsgate CT12 24 B1

Radley Cl CT10 23 G2
Radnor Cl CT6 12 D5
Raglan Pl CT10 5 C4
Railway Av CT5 9 F3
Railway Ter CT9 3 B4
Ramsey Cl CT2 35 E1
Ramsgate Rd, Broadstairs CT10 5 A5
Ramsgate Rd, Margate CT9 19 G4
Ramsgate Rd, Sandwich CT13 29 F1
Rancorn Rd CT9 18 D3
Randolph Cl CT1 35 G3
Randolph Sq CT9 3 F1
Ranelagh Gro CT10 23 E3
Ransome Way CT7 16 D5
Rattington St CT4 39 C2
Ravensbourne Av CT6 12 D4
Ravenscourt Rd CT2 30 B5
Rawdon Rd CT11 24 C4
Rayham Rd CT5 9 H4
Raymond Av CT11 35 G3
Reading St CT10 21 E6
Reading Street Rd CT10 20 D5
Rectory Gdns CT5 10 C3
Rectory Rd CT10 5 C2
Reculver Av CT7 16 C3
Reculver Cl CT6 13 H1
Reculver Dr CT6 13 G1
Reculver Rd CT6 13 E3
Reculvers Rd CT8 18 A5
Red Lion La*, Sea St CT5 9 E2
Redcot La CT2 33 F1
Redhill Rd CT8 17 H3
Redwood Cl CT2 31 E6
Reed Av CT1 32 A5
Reeds Cl CT6 13 E2
Reeves Way CT5 10 B5
Regency Cl CT5 9 G4
Regency Pl CT1 31 H6
Regent St CT5 9 E2
Regents Walk CT6 13 F2
Remston Mews*, Military Rd CT1 31 H6
Renault Cl CT6 11 F2
Rentain Rd CT4 39 C2
Repton Cl CT10 23 E2
Reservoir Rd CT5 9 F1
Reynolds Cl CT6 12 D2
Rheims Ct CT2 34 D1
Rheims Way CT1 6 A4
Rhodaus Cl CT1 6 B5
Rhodaus Town CT1 6 B5
Rhodes Gdns CT10 23 F2
Richardson Way CT12 26 B5
Richborough Rd, Sandwich CT13 29 E1
Richborough Rd, Westgate on Sea CT8 18 A5
Richmond Av CT9 20 A4
Richmond Dr CT6 13 H2
Richmond Gdns CT2 30 B6
Richmond Rd, Ramsgate CT11 4 B2
Richmond Rd, Whitstable CT5 10 A5
Richmond St CT6 12 B1
Ridgeway CT5 10 A5
Ridgeway Cliff CT6 11 H1
Ridgeway Rd CT6 14 C2
Ridgeway Walk CT6 14 D2
Ridley Cl CT6 12 C6
Riley Av CT6 11 E2
Ringold Av CT12 24 B2
Ringwood Cl CT2 31 E5
Risdon Cl CT2 32 D1
River Cl CT4 39 B1
River Vw CT2 32 D1
Riverdale Rd CT1 31 H5
Riverhead Cl CT9 20 B4
Rivers Ct CT12 15 C6
Riverside CT4 39 B1
Riverside Cl CT4 37 B5
Riverside Mews CT4 37 B5
Roberts Rd CT5 8 B6
Rochester Av CT1 35 H3
Rockingham Pl CT6 13 E5
Rockstone Way CT12 24 B1
Rodney St CT11 4 B3
Roman Rd CT12 22 B6
Romilly Gdns CT12 22 C6

Romney Cl CT7 17 E4
Roper Cl CT2 6 A1
Roper Rd CT2 6 A2
Rose Acre Rd CT3 38 A3
Rose Gdns,
  Birchington CT7 16 D5
Rose Gdns,
  Herne Bay CT6 13 E2
Rose Gdns,
  Ramsgate CT12 15 B5
Rose Hill CT11 4 C2
Rose La CT1 6 C4
Roseacre Cl CT2 35 E1
Roseacre Ct CT9 20 D3
Rosebery Av,
  Herne Bay CT6 13 G2
Rosebery Av,
  Ramsgate CT11 25 G2
Rosedale Rd CT9 19 H3
Roselands Gdns
  CT2 30 B6
Roselawn Gdns CT9 18 C4
Roselea Av CT6 12 C4
Rosemary Av CT10 5 A6
Rosemary Gdns,
  Broadstairs CT10 23 F6
Rosemary Gdns,
  Whitstable CT5 9 H4
Rosemary La CT1 6 A4
Rosetower Ct CT10 21 E5
Ross Gdns CT2 30 B5
Rossetti Rd CT7 16 D5
Rossland Rd CT12 24 B2
Rothsay Ct*,
  Argyll Dr CT11 25 G1
Rough Common Rd
  CT2 30 B6
Rowan Cl CT2 32 D2
Rowan Ct CT10 5 A2
Rowe Cl CT9 19 G5
Rowena Rd CT8 17 H1
Rowland Cres CT6 13 G2
Rowland Dr CT6 11 G4
Roxburgh Rd CT8 18 A4
Royal Av CT5 7 C1
Royal Cl CT10 23 E4
Royal Cres,
  Margate CT9 3 A3
Royal Cres,
  Ramsgate CT11 4 B4
Royal Esplanade,
  Margate CT9 18 B3
Royal Esplanade,
  Ramsgate CT11 24 C6
Royal Harbour App
  CT11 24 C6
Royal Par CT11 25 F5
Royal Rd CT11 4 B3
Rugby Cl CT10 23 E3
Rumfields Rd CT10 22 C4
Runcie Pl*,
  Bishops Way CT2 34 D1
Rushmead Cl CT2 31 E6
Russell Dr CT5 10 C3
Russett Rd CT1 36 A3
Rutland Av CT9 20 B3
Rutland Cl CT1 36 B3
Rutland Gdns,
  Birchington CT7 16 D3
Rutland Gdns,
  Margate CT9 20 B3
Rydal Av CT11 24 B4
Ryde St CT2 35 E1
Ryders Av CT8 17 H2
Rye Walk CT6 13 F5

Sacketts Gap CT9 20 C2
Sacketts Hill CT10 22 B2
Saddlers Mews CT5 10 C4
Saddleton Gro CT5 9 E4
Saddleton Rd CT5 9 E4
St Albans Rd CT3 38 C4
St Alphege Cl CT5 8 C5
St Alphege La CT1 6 C2
St Andrews Cl,
  Canterbury CT1 6 A5
St Andrews Cl,
  Herne Bay CT6 12 C3
St Andrews Cl,
  Margate CT9 19 G5
St Andrews Cl,
  Whitstable CT5 9 F5
St Andrews Lees
  CT13 29 F3
St Andrews Rd CT11 25 G2
St Annes Dr CT6 12 A3
St Annes Gdns CT9 19 G5
St Annes Rd CT5 9 G1
St Anthonys Way

CT9 20 B4
St Augustines Av
  CT9 19 G5
St Augustines Cres
  CT5 10 C3
St Augustines Pk
  CT11 24 D5
St Augustines Rd,
  Canterbury CT1 35 H3
St Augustines Rd,
  Ramsgate CT11 4 A4
St Barts Rd CT13 29 E3
St Benedicts Lawn
  CT11 4 A4
St Benets Rd CT8 18 A5
St Catherines Ct*,
  Argyll Dr CT11 25 F1
St Catherines Gro
  CT12 26 D2
St Christopher Cl
  CT9 20 C5
St Christophers Grn
  CT10 23 F3
St Clements CT13 29 F2
St Clements Rd CT8 18 A3
St Crispins Rd CT8 18 A5
St Davids Cl,
  Birchington CT7 17 F3
St Davids Cl,
  Whitstable CT5 9 G4
St Davids Rd CT11 25 G2
St Dunstans Cl CT2 35 E1
St Dunstans Rd CT9 20 A4
St Dunstans St CT2 35 E1
St Dunstans Ter CT2 35 E1
St Edmunds Rd CT1 6 B4
St Francis Cl CT9 20 C5
St Georges CT5 9 F5
St Georges Av CT6 11 H2
St Georges La CT1 6 C5
St Georges Lees
  CT13 29 F2
St Georges Pl CT1 6 D4
St Georges Rd,
  Broadstairs CT10 5 A4
St Georges Rd,
  Ramsgate CT11 25 G2
St Georges Rd,
  Sandwich CT13 29 F3
St Georges St CT1 6 C4
St Georges Ter,
  Canterbury CT1 6 C5
St Georges Ter,
  Herne Bay CT6 12 A2
St Gregorys Rd CT1 35 H1
St Jacobs Pl CT1 35 E4
St James Av,
  Broadstairs CT10 23 E3
St James Av,
  Ramsgate CT12 24 C1
St James Gdns CT5 9 E4
St James Park Rd
  CT9 18 B4
St James Ter CT7 17 F2
St Jeans Rd CT8 18 A6
St Johns Av East
  CT12 24 B1
St Johns Av West
  CT12 24 A1
St Johns Cres CT2 31 E1
St Johns La CT1 6 B4
St Johns Pl CT1 6 D1
St Johns Rd,
  Margate CT9 3 D3
St Johns Rd,
  Whitstable CT5 10 C3
St Johns St CT9 3 D3
St Julien Av CT1 36 B1
St Lawrence CT11 24 D3
St Lawrence Av CT11 24 C6
St Lawrence Cl CT1 35 H3
St Lawrence Forstal
  CT1 35 H4
St Lawrence Rd CT1 35 H4
St Louis Gro CT6 11 H1
St Lukes Av CT11 25 E2
St Lukes Cl,
  Westgate on Sea
  CT8 18 A5
St Lukes Cl,
  Whitstable CT5 9 F5
St Lukes Rd CT11 25 F3
St Magnus Rd CT10 16 D2
St Magnus Ct*,
  St Magnus Cl CT7 17 E2
St Margarets Rd CT8 18 A5
St Margarets St CT1 6 B4
St Marks Cl CT5 9 F4

St Martins Av CT1 35 H2
St Martins Cl CT1 35 H2
St Martins Hill CT1 36 A2
St Martins Pl CT1 35 H2
St Martins Rd CT1 35 H2
St Martins Ter CT1 35 H2
St Martins Vw CT6 12 D6
St Marys Av CT9 20 C4
St Marys Cl,
  Eastry CT13 27 C5
St Marys Cl,
  Woodnesborough
  CT13 28 A5
St Marys Ct CT6 12 B3
St Marys Gro CT5 8 A6
St Marys Rd,
  Broadstairs CT10 5 C3
St Marys Rd,
  Canterbury CT4 37 C3
St Marys Rd,
  Ramsgate CT12 15 B5
St Marys St CT1 6 B4
St Michaels Alley
  CT11 4 C2
St Michaels Av CT10 20 C5
St Michaels Cl CT2 30 B6
St Michaels Pl CT2 31 E6
St Michaels Rd CT2 31 E5
St Mildreds Av,
  Birchington CT7 16 C3
St Mildreds Av,
  Broadstairs CT10 5 A4
St Mildreds Av,
  Ramsgate CT11 24 D6
St Mildreds Ct*,
  St Peters Pl CT1 6 A3
St Mildreds Gdns
  CT8 18 B3
St Mildreds Pl CT11 35 E3
St Mildreds Rd,
  Margate CT9 20 A4
St Mildreds Rd,
  Minster CT12 15 B6
St Mildreds Rd,
  Ramsgate CT11 24 D5
St Mildreds Rd,
  Westgate on Sea
  CT8 18 A4
St Nicholas Cl CT2 32 D1
St Nicholas Rd CT1 34 D4
St Patricks Cl CT5 9 F5
St Patricks Rd CT11 25 G2
St Pauls Rd CT9 19 H2
St Pauls Ter CT1 6 D4
St Peters Ct CT10 23 F3
St Peters Footpath
  CT9 3 E4
St Peters Gro CT1 6 A3
St Peters La CT1 6 B3
St Peters Park Rd
  CT10 5 A1
St Peters Pl CT1 6 A3
St Peters Rd,
  Broadstairs CT10 23 E3
St Peters Rd,
  Margate CT9 3 E4
St Peters St,
  Canterbury CT1 6 B2
St Peters St,
  Sandwich CT13 29 F1
St Peters St,
  Whitstable CT5 9 E2
St Radigunds Pl CT1 6 C1
St Stephens Cl CT2 31 F6
St Stephens Ct CT2 31 F6
St Stephens Fields*,
  CT2 31 F6
St Stephens Footpath
  CT2 31 F6
St Stephens Grn CT2 31 F5
St Stephens Hill CT2 31 E3
St Stephens Rd CT2 6 B1
St Swithins Rd CT5 10 A4
St Thomas Hill CT2 30 C5
St Vincents Cl,
  Canterbury CT3 38 A1
St Vincents Cl,
  Whitstable CT5 9 F5
Salisbury Av,
  Broadstairs CT10 23 F5
Salisbury Av,
  Ramsgate CT11 25 F3
Salisbury Rd,
  Canterbury CT2 31 E5
Salisbury Rd,
  Herne Bay CT6 13 E2
Salisbury Rd,
  Whitstable CT5 9 E4
Salmestone Rd CT9 19 G5

Salt Marsh La CT5 9 E2
Salts Cl CT5 9 E3
Salts Dr CT10 23 E3
Saltwood Gdns CT9 20 D3
Sancroft Av CT2 34 D1
Sanctuary Cl CT10 23 F6
Sandalwood Dr CT7 14 C6
Sandend CT5 8 D6
Sandhurst Cl CT2 31 G4
Sandhurst Rd CT9 21 E3
Sandles Rd CT7 16 D3
Sandown Dr CT6 12 A2
Sandown Lees CT13 29 H3
Sandown Rd CT13 29 F2
Sandpiper Rd CT5 8 C6
Sandwich By-Pass
  CT13 28 C2
Sandwich Rd,
  Ash CT3 27 C2
Sandwich Rd,
  Eastry CT13 27 C5
Sandwich Rd,
  Ramsgate CT12 26 C6
Sandwich Rd,
  Woodnesborough
  CT13 28 C4
Sandwood Rd,
  Sandwich CT13 29 E2
Sanger Cl CT9 19 F4
Sangro Pl CT1 36 B1
Sarah Gdns CT9 20 C5
Sarre Pl CT13 29 E3
Saunders La CT3 27 D3
Savernake Dr CT6 12 D5
Saxon Rd,
  Canterbury CT4 37 B5
Saxon Rd,
  Ramsgate CT11 24 C5
Saxon Rd,
  Westgate on Sea
  CT8 18 B4
Saxon Shore CT5 8 D3
Sceales Dr CT12 26 B5
Sceptre Way CT5 8 D5
School La,
  Bekesbourne CT4 37 D1
School La, Blean CT2 30 A1
School La,
  Herne Bay CT6 12 D6
School La,
  Littlebourne CT3 38 D2
School La,
  Ramsgate CT11 4 D1
School La, Sturry CT2 33 E4
School Rd,
  Canterbury CT3 27 B2
School Rd,
  Sandwich CT13 29 E1
Sea Approach CT10 5 C3
Sea Rd CT7,8 17 F2
Sea St,
  Herne Bay CT6 11 G2
Sea St,
  Whitstable CT5 9 E2
Sea View Av CT7 16 C2
Sea View Rd,
  Birchington CT7 16 C2
Sea View Rd,
  Broadstairs CT10 23 G2
Sea View Rd,
  Herne Bay CT6 13 E1
Sea View Rd,
  Ramsgate CT12 26 C5
Sea View Sq CT6 12 B1
Sea View Ter CT9 19 E3
Sea Wall CT5 9 E2
Seacroft Rd CT10 25 H1
Seafield Rd,
  Broadstairs CT10 5 A4
Seafield Rd,
  Ramsgate CT11 24 D4
Seafield Rd,
  Whitstable CT5 10 A3
Seamark Rd CT7 16 C6
Seapoint Rd CT10 5 C5
Seasalter Beach CT5 8 C5
Seasalter La CT5 7 A2
Seaville Dr CT6 13 G1
Second Av,
  Broadstairs CT10 21 F3
Second Av,
  Margate CT9 20 A2
Seeshill Cl CT5 9 F4
Selbey Cl CT6 13 F3
Selborne Rd CT9 20 A5
Selsea Av CT6 11 H1
Selwyn Dr CT10 23 E3

Semaphore Rd CT7
Semple Cl CT12
Senlac Cl CT11
Setterfield Rd CT10
Sevastopol Pl CT1
Seven Posts Alley*,
  St Peters St CT13
Seven Stones Dr
  CT10
Sewell Cl CT7
Seymour Av,
  Margate CT9
Seymour Av,
  Whitstable CT5
Seymour Cl CT6
Seymour Pl CT1
Shaftesbury Rd,
  Canterbury CT2
Shaftesbury Rd,
  Hersden CT3
Shaftesbury Rd,
  Whitstable CT5
Shaftsbury St CT11
Shah Pl*,
  Station Approach
  CT11
Shakespeare Passag
Shakespeare Rd,
  Birchington CT7
Shakespeare Rd,
  Margate CT9
Shalloak Rd CT2
Shallows Rd CT10
Shalmsford Ct CT4
Shalmsford St CT4
Shamrock Av CT5
Shapland Cl CT6
Share and Coulter R
  CT5
Shearwater Av CT5
Shelley Av CT1
Shepherds Walk CT?
Shepherds Way CT5
Shepherdsgate CT2
Shepherdsgate Dr
  CT2
Sheppey Cl CT7
Sheppey Vw CT5
Sherwood Cl,
  Herne Bay CT6
Sherwood Cl,
  Whitstable CT5
Sherwood Dr CT5
Sherwood Gdns CT?
Sherwood Rd CT7
Shipman Av CT2
Shipwrights Lee CT?
Shirley Av CT11
Shore Cl CT6
Short St CT13
Shottendane Rd CT9
Shuart La CT7
Shutler Rd CT10
Sidney Pl*,
  Market St CT9
Silver Av CT7
Silverdale Dr CT6
Silverdale Rd CT11
Simmonds Rd CT1
Simon Av CT9
Singer Av CT6
Singleton Cl CT12
Sion Hill CT11
Slades Cl CT5
Sleigh Rd CT2
Sloe La CT9
Smugglers Way CT7
Snell Gdns CT6
Sobraon Way CT1
Somerset Cl CT5
Somerset Cl CT10
Somerset Rd CT1
Somme Cl CT1
Somner Cl CT1
Sondes Cl CT6
South Canterbury Rd
  CT1
South Cl CT11
South Cliff Par CT10
South Eastern Rd
  CT11
South Lodge Cl CT5
South Rd CT6
South St,
  Canterbury CT1
South St,
  Whitstable CT5
South View Rd CT5

ll Cl CT12	15 B4
ea Dr CT6	12 A3
old Pl CT8	17 H3
ood Gdns	
	24 C4
ood Rd,	
sgate CT11	24 D4
ood Rd,	
stable CT5	10 A4
St CT10	23 F3
planade CT6	11 G1
w Castle CT9	3 E4
Rd CT10	23 E2
urst Gdns	
	21 E2
r Rd CT7	16 D2
r Sq CT11	4 B4
r St CT11	4 C3
r Rd CT6	12 B3
v CT5	9 H4
g La CT12	24 A1
g St CT12	24 A1
La,	
erbury CT1	35 H2
La,	
wich CT2	32 D4
Walk CT5	9 E5
ield Cl,	
dstairs CT10	23 E6
ield Cl,	
sgate CT11	25 F1
ield Rd CT9	20 D2
Av CT2	34 D2
dshire St CT11	4 D1
Hill CT2	33 E1
Pl,	
dstairs CT10	5 C2
Pl,	
erbury CT1	6 C4
mb Av CT11	24 D5
rd Av CT6	11 F2
Ct CT12	24 B3
Gdns CT6	12 C3
Pl,	
dstairs CT10	5 B3
Pl,	
sgate CT11	25 E3
Rd,	
dstairs CT10	23 F2
Rd,	
e Bay CT6	12 C3
Rd,	
ate CT9	19 H2
Rd,	
sgate CT11	25 E3
Rd,	
stable CT5	9 E4
Sykes Cl CT9	20 A5
re Ct CT7	35 H3
urst Av CT10	23 G6
urst Gdns	
	21 E3
CT9	22 A3
Cl CT1	31 G6
orough La	
	27 B4
App,	
ington CT7	16 D3
App,	
ate CT9	3 B3
App,	
sgate CT12	15 B6
Approach Rd	
	25 E3
Chine CT6	12 B3
Par CT7	16 D3
Rd,	
sbourne CT4	37 C2
Rd,	
ington CT7	16 D3
e CT4	37 A5
Rd,	
e Bay CT6	12 B2
Rd,	
ate CT9	3 A3
Rd,	
sgate CT12	15 B6
gate on Sea	
	18 A4
Rd,	
stable CT5	9 F1
Rd East CT1	6 A5
Rd West CT2	6 A2
Cl CT6	14 D1
n CT10	5 B4
n Cl CT10	23 G4
ns Cl CT9	18 C5

Stephens Cl CT12	24 D2
Stephenson Rd CT2	31 F5
Sterling Cl CT10	23 E3
Steven Ct CT11	24 C6
Stirling Way CT12	24 B1
Stockbury Gdns CT9	20 D3
Stodmarsh Rd CT3	33 E6
Stonar Cl,	
Ramsgate CT11	25 F1
Stonar Cl,	
Sandwich CT13	29 F1
Stonar Gdns CT13	29 F1
Stonar Rd CT13	29 F1
Stone Barn Av CT7	17 E4
Stone Cross Lees	
CT13	29 E3
Stone Gdns CT10	5 C2
Stone Rd CT10	5 C2
Stour Cl CT4	39 C2
Stour Cres CT1	32 B5
Stour Ct CT13	29 E2
Stour Rd CT4	39 C2
Stour St CT1	6 A4
Stour Villas CT1	6 B4
Strand St CT13	29 E1
Strangers Cl CT1	34 C4
Strangers La CT1	34 C4
Strangford Pl CT6	13 E5
Strangford Rd CT5	9 G2
Strasbourg St CT9	22 A2
Stream Walk CT5	9 F2
Streete Court Rd CT8	18 A5
Streete Ct CT8	18 A5
Streetfield CT6	12 D6
Stringer Dr CT7	17 E5
Strode Park Rd CT6	12 C5
Stuart Ct CT1	35 G4
Studds Cotts CT6	11 F3
Stuppington Court Fm	
CT1	35 E6
Stuppington La CT1	35 E6
Sturmer Ct CT1	36 A2
Sturry Court Mews	
CT2	32 C2
Sturry Hill CT2	32 C2
Sturry Rd CT1,2	31 G6
Sudbury Pl CT8	17 H3
Suffolk Av CT8	17 H3
Suffolk Rd CT1	36 B2
Suffolk St CT5	9 E4
Summer Ct CT2	34 C1
Summer Hill CT2	34 C1
Summer La CT2	31 E2
Summer Rd CT7	14 B6
Summerfield Av CT5	9 G2
Summerfield Rd CT9	21 E3
Sun La CT7	14 B5
Sun St CT1	6 C3
Sunbeam Av CT6	11 F2
Sundew Gro CT11	25 F3
Sundridge Cl CT2	31 G4
Sunningdale Walk	
CT6	11 H4
Sunnyhill Rd CT6	11 G2
Sunnymead CT2	30 D1
Sunnyside Gdns	
CT13	11 H4
Sunnyside Rd CT5	7 D1
Sunray Av CT5	8 C5
Sunset Cl CT5	8 D6
Surrey Gdns CT7	16 D3
Surrey Rd,	
Canterbury CT1	36 B3
Surrey Rd,	
Margate CT9	20 B2
Sussex Av,	
Canterbury CT1	36 A3
Sussex Av,	
Margate CT9	19 G4
Sussex Cl CT10	11 G2
Sussex Gdns,	
Birchington CT7	16 D3
Sussex Gdns,	
Herne Bay CT6	11 G2
Sussex Gdns,	
Westgate on Sea	
CT8	18 A3
Sussex St CT11	25 F3
Sutherland Dr CT7	17 E4
Sutton Rd CT3	38 D4
Swakeley Walk CT5	10 B3
Swale Cl CT6	12 D4
Swalecliffe Av CT5	9 F1
Swalecliffe Court Dr	
CT5	10 C3
Swalecliffe Rd CT5	10 A4
Swallow Av CT5	8 D5
Swallow Cl CT10	19 E4
Swanfield Rd CT5	9 E3

Swanton La CT3	33 G6
Swaynes Way CT13	27 B6
Sweechbridge Rd	
CT6	13 H3
Sweyn Rd CT9	19 H2
Swinburne Av CT10	5 A5
Swinford Gdns CT9	20 C5
Sycamore Cl,	
Broadstairs CT10	22 C4
Sycamore Cl,	
Herne Bay CT6	13 F2
Sycamore Cl,	
Margate CT9	19 F5
Sydenham St CT5	9 E2
Sydney Cooper Cl	
CT2	30 B6
Sydney Rd,	
Ramsgate CT11	25 G3
Sydney Rd,	
Whitstable CT5	9 F4
Taddy Gdns CT9	20 C5
Talavera Rd CT1	36 A1
Talbot Av CT6	11 F2
Talbot Rd CT9	20 A4
Tankerton Heights	
CT5	9 F1
Tankerton Mews CT5	9 F1
Tankerton Rd CT5	9 F1
Tassells Walk CT5	10 C3
Tavistock Rd CT11	25 E1
Taylor Rd CT12	15 B5
Teddington Cl CT1	31 H6
Telford St CT6	12 B1
Telham Av CT12	24 C3
Temple Rd CT2	34 D1
Temple Way CT14	29 F6
Ten Perch Rd CT1	34 D4
Tennyson Av CT1	32 A5
Tenterden Dr CT2	31 F4
Tenterden Way CT9	20 B5
Terminus Dr CT6	13 F2
Terrys La CT5	9 E2
Teynham Cl CT9	21 E3
Teynham Dr CT5	9 G2
Teynham Rd CT5	9 G2
Thanet Cl CT10	5 C2
Thanet Place Gdns	
CT10	23 H2
Thanet Rd,	
Broadstairs CT10	5 C3
Thanet Rd,	
Margate CT9	3 E3
Thanet Rd,	
Ramsgate CT11	25 G3
Thanet Rd,	
Westgate on Sea	
CT8	17 H2
Thanet Way,	
Herne Bay CT6	11 E3
Thanet Way,	
St Nicholas at Wade	
CT7	14 A4
Thanet Way,	
Whitstable CT5	7 A3
Thanington Rd CT1	34 C4
The Avenue,	
Canterbury CT3	38 C4
The Avenue,	
Margate CT9	19 H3
The Banks CT10	23 F2
The Borough CT1	6 C2
The Boundary CT1	34 D4
The Bridge App CT5	9 G2
The Broadway,	
Broadstairs CT10	5 A3
The Broadway,	
Herne Bay CT6	11 G1
The Broadway,	
Ramsgate CT11	4 B3
The Butchery*,	
Market St CT13	29 F1
The Butts CT13	29 E1
The Causeway,	
Canterbury CT2	6 B1
The Causeway,	
Sandwich CT13	28 C1
The Chain CT13	29 F2
The Circus CT6	12 A3
The Cloisters CT11	4 B4
The Close,	
Bridge CT4	37 A5
The Close,	
Downs Rd CT2	31 F4
The Close*,	
Cockering Rd CT1	34 D4
The Coppice CT2	32 D2
The Courts CT9	18 B4
The Crescent,	

Canterbury CT2	31 F4
The Crescent,	
Chartham CT4	39 C3
The Crescent,	
Sandwich CT13	28 D5
The Cuttings CT12	24 D2
The Dene CT1	35 H5
The Downings CT6	12 D4
The Downs CT4	39 C3
The Drive,	
Canterbury CT1	35 H4
The Drive,	
Whitstable CT5	10 C5
The Drove,	
Canterbury CT2	32 D4
The Drove,	
Whitstable CT5	10 C6
The Elders CT3	38 A1
The Elms CT3	38 D4
The Fairway CT6	12 A5
The Finches CT7	14 B5
The Footpath CT10	5 C3
The Foreland CT1	35 H5
The Friars CT1	6 B3
The Gap, Blean CT2	30 A1
The Gap,	
Canterbury CT1	35 H5
The Grange CT5	8 B6
The Green,	
Blean CT2	30 A2
The Green,	
Chartham CT4	39 C1
The Green,	
Littlebourne CT3	38 B3
The Green,	
Ramsgate CT12	26 D2
The Grove,	
Herne Bay CT6	11 H4
The Grove,	
Westgate on Sea	
CT8	18 A4
The Halt CT5	9 H5
The Hamele CT2	32 C3
The Hawthorns CT10	22 C4
The Heath CT5	10 A5
The Heights CT5	8 D5
The Hill CT3	38 A2
The Horshams CT6	13 G2
The Hoystings Cl CT1	6 D6
The Hyde CT4	39 A2
The Lanes CT12	15 C5
The Larches CT5	9 E4
The Leas,	
Whitstable CT5	10 B5
The Lees,	
Herne Bay CT6	13 E1
The Lees,	
Herne Bay CT6	13 F1
The Length CT7	14 B5
The Malthouses CT7	16 D3
The Maltings CT3	38 B3
The Maples CT10	22 C4
The Meadows CT6	13 F4
The Mint CT2	34 C1
The Ness CT1	35 G5
The New Cl CT4	37 B4
The Nook CT12	22 C5
The Oaks,	
Birchington CT7	14 B5
The Oaks,	
Broadstairs CT10	21 E6
The Oaks,	
Canterbury CT3	38 D4
The Oaze CT5	8 D6
The Paddock CT1	35 H2
The Paddocks,	
Broadstairs CT10	21 F6
The Paddocks,	
Herne Bay CT6	13 H2
The Parade,	
Birchington CT7	16 B3
The Parade,	
Broadstairs CT10	5 C3
The Parade,	
Canterbury CT1	6 C3
The Parade,	
Margate CT9	3 D2
The Parkway CT7	17 E4
The Passage CT9	3 F1
The Pathway CT10	5 C3
The Pines CT10	22 C4
The Poplars CT3	38 D4
The Promenade	
CT10	23 H5
The Quay CT5	29 F2
The Rendezvous CT9	3 D1
The Retreat,	
Birchington CT7	17 E2
The Retreat,	

Ramsgate CT12	24 C2
The Ridgeway,	
Broadstairs CT10	23 E5
The Ridgeway,	
Margate CT9	20 B4
The Ridings,	
Margate CT9	20 D2
The Ridings,	
Whitstable CT5	10 C5
The Russets CT5	10 C5
The Saltings CT5	9 E2
The School Cl CT8	17 H1
The Silvers CT10	22 C4
The Spinney CT9	20 D4
The Square CT7	17 E4
The Street,	
Birchington CT7	14 B5
The Street,	
Deal CT14	29 F6
The Street,	
Eastry CT3	27 B2
The Street,	
Littlebourne CT3	38 D1
The Street,	
Patrixbourne CT4	37 C3
The Street,	
Sandwich CT13	28 B4
The Sycamores CT3	38 C4
The Terrace CT2	31 F5
The Vale CT10	5 A4
The Vespers CT2	6 B1
The Warren CT5	9 E6
The Warren Dr CT8	17 G3
Third Av CT9	20 A2
Thirlmere Av CT11	24 B4
Thorn Gdns CT11	25 F1
Thornden Cl CT6	11 F3
Thornden Ct CT2	30 C4
Thornden Wood Rd	
CT6	11 F6
Thorne Rd CT12	15 B5
Thornton La CT13	27 A6
Three Kings Alley*,	
St Peters St CT13	29 F2
Throwley Dr CT6	11 H2
Thruxted La CT4	39 A3
Thundersland Rd	
CT6	12 D3
Thurlow Av CT6	13 E1
Thurston Pk CT5	9 F3
Tile Kiln Hill CT2	30 B3
Tina Gdns CT10	23 G2
Tippledore La CT10	23 E3
Tivoli Brook CT9	19 F4
Tivoli Park Av CT9	3 B4
Tivoli Rd CT9	19 F5
Tollemache Cl CT12	26 A2
Tollgate Cl CT5	9 E4
Tomlin Dr CT9	20 C6
Tomsons Passage	
CT11	4 B1
Tonford La CT1	34 B4
Tothill St CT12	15 B5
Tourtel Rd CT1	31 G6
Tower Bungalows*,	
Spencer Rd CT7	17 E2
Tower Gdns CT6	12 B1
Tower Hill CT5	9 F1
Tower Par CT5	9 F1
Tower Rd CT5	9 F1
Tower Vw CT4	39 D3
Tower Way CT1	6 B3
Townley St CT11	4 B3
Treasury Vw CT3	38 D2
Trinity Hill CT9	3 D2
Trinity Pl CT11	25 G3
Trinity Sq,	
Broadstairs CT10	21 F6
Trinity Sq,	
Margate CT9	3 E1
Troughton Mews CT9	3 A4
Trove Ct CT11	4 E1
Trueman Cl CT2	30 A1
Truro Rd CT11	4 F1
Tudor Cl CT7	17 F3
Tudor Ct CT2	30 C4
Tudor Rd CT1	6 A6
Tunis Ct CT1	36 B1
Tunis Row CT10	5 C2
Tunstall Rd CT2	31 G4
Turnagain La CT1	6 C3
Turnden Gdns CT9	20 D3
Turner St CT11	4 D2
Twyne Cl CT2	32 D2
Tydemans Av CT5	10 B5
Tyler Cl CT2	31 F5
Tyler Hill Rd CT2	30 A2
Tyler Way CT5	10 D3
Tyndale Pk CT6	12 D2

Tyson Av CT9 18 B4
Ulcombe Gdns CT2 31 G4
Ulster Rd CT9 19 G4
Underdown La CT6 12 C4
Underdown Rd CT6 12 C2
Underwood Cl CT1 35 G5
Union Cres CT9 3 D3
Union Pl CT1 6 D1
Union Rd,
  Canterbury CT4 37 A5
Union Rd,
  Ramsgate CT11 25 G2
Union Row CT9 3 D2
Union Sq CT10 5 D3
Union St,
  Canterbury CT1 6 D2
Union St,
  Ramsgate CT11 4 D1
Unity Pl CT11 25 G3
University Rd CT2 30 D5
Upchurch Walk CT9 21 E4
Uplands CT2 31 F4
Upper Approach Rd
  CT10 5 B5
Upper Bridge St CT1 6 C5
Upper Chantry La CT1 6 D5
Upper Dane Rd CT9 20 A4
Upper Dumpton Rd
  CT11 25 F3
Upper Free Down
  CT6 12 D4
Upper Gore La CT13 27 A6
Upper Gro CT9 3 E3
Upper Maltings Pl
  CT7 16 D3
Upper Strand St
  CT13 29 F2
Upton Rd CT10 23 F3
Ursuline Dr CT8 17 G3

Vale Pl CT11 4 A2
Vale Rd,
  Broadstairs CT10 23 E4
Vale Rd,
  Ramsgate CT11 24 D4
Vale Rd,
  Whitstable CT5 9 F4
Vale Sq CT11 4 A3
Vale Ter CT11 4 A2
Valkyrie Av CT5 8 D4
Valley Rd,
  Broadstairs CT10 22 C1
Valley Rd,
  Canterbury CT1 35 E4
Vauxhall Av,
  Canterbury CT1 32 A4
Vauxhall Av,
  Herne Bay CT6 11 F2
Vauxhall Cres CT1 32 A4
Vauxhall Industrial Rd
  CT1 32 A4
Vauxhall Rd CT1 32 A4
Ventnor La CT9 3 E4
Vere Rd CT10 5 B3
Vereth Rd CT11 4 A3
Vernon Pl CT1 6 D5
Verwood Cl CT2 31 E5
Vesty Ct CT8 18 A3
Viaduct Cl CT12 24 D2
Vicarage Cres CT9 19 G4
Vicarage La,
  Canterbury CT2 30 B2
Vicarage La,
  Sandwich CT13 29 E1
Vicarage Pl CT9 3 D4
Vicarage St CT10 22 D3
Victor Av CT9 20 D3
Victoria Av,
  Broadstairs CT10 20 D6
Victoria Av,
  Margate CT9 20 A4
Victoria Av,
  Westgate on Sea
  CT8 18 A5
Victoria Dr CT6 11 H1
Victoria Par,
  Broadstairs CT10 5 C5
Victoria Par,
  Ramsgate CT11 24 D4
Victoria Pk CT6 12 C2
Victoria Rd,

Broadstairs CT10 23 E2
Victoria Rd,
  Canterbury CT1 35 E3
Victoria Rd,
  Margate CT9 3 E4
Victoria Rd,
  Ramsgate CT11 25 F3
Victoria Row CT1 6 D2
Victoria St CT5 9 E2
Victory Ct CT1 6 A6
Viking Cl CT7 16 B3
Viking Ct CT10 5 C6
Villiers Rd CT1 36 B1
Vincent Cl CT12 22 C5
Vine Cl CT11 22 D6
Vinten Cl CT6 14 D1
Violet Av CT12 22 C6
Virginia Rd CT5 9 H4
Vulcan Cl CT5 9 E4

Wacher Cl CT2 31 F6
Waldron Rd CT10 23 G6
Walker La CT7 16 B2
Wallace Way CT10 23 E4
Wallwood Rd CT11 25 G2
Walmer Gdns CT12 26 B6
Walmer Rd CT5 9 F4
Walmsley Rd CT10 5 A2
Walnut Tree Cl CT7 17 E4
Walnut Tree La,
  Canterbury CT2 33 G1
Walnut Tree La,
  Westbere CT3 38 B6
Walpole Rd CT9 3 E2
Waltham Cl CT9 21 E3
Wantsum Cl CT6 13 H1
Wantsum Mews*,
  Loop St CT13 29 E1
Wantsum Way CT7 14 B5
Wantsume Lees
  CT13 28 D1
Wardour Cl CT10 5 C3
Warre Av CT11 24 D5
Warren Dr CT10 23 E3
Warten Rd CT11 25 G1
Warwick Dr CT11 24 C5
Warwick Rd,
  Canterbury CT1 36 A2
Warwick Rd,
  Margate CT9 20 B3
Warwick Rd,
  Whitstable CT5 9 E2
Watchester Av CT11 4 A4
Watchester La CT12 15 B6
Water La,
  Canterbury CT1 6 B4
Water La, Sturry CT2 32 D3
Water Mdws CT2 32 D3
Waterloo Pl CT11 4 E1
Waterloo Rd CT5 9 E2
Waterside Dr CT8 18 A3
Watling St CT1 6 B4
Watts Yd CT13 29 E2
Wauchope Rd CT5 8 B5
Wave Crest CT5 8 D3
Waverley Rd CT9 18 D4
Way Hill CT12 15 D5
Wayborough Hill
  CT12 15 D5
Wayne Cl CT10 23 E3
Wealdhurst Pk CT10 22 D3
Weatherly Dr CT10 23 F6
Weddington La CT13 27 C1
Weigall Pl CT11 24 C4
Well Cl CT2 33 E1
Well La CT2 32 D4
Wellesley Cl,
  Broadstairs CT10 23 E5
Wellesley Cl,
  Westgate on Sea
  CT8 18 A6
Wellesley Rd,
  Margate CT9 20 A4
Wellesley Rd,
  Westgate on Sea
  CT8 18 A5
Wellington Cres CT11 4 E2
Wellington Rd CT8 18 A5
Wellington St CT5 7 D1
Wellis Gdns CT9 19 E4
Wells Av CT1 35 H3

Welsdene Rd CT9 18 C5
Wemyss Way CT1 36 A2
Wentworth Av CT9 18 B4
Wentworth Dr CT12 24 B2
Wentworth Gdns CT6 12 A5
West Beach CT5 8 D3
West Cliff CT5 9 E3
West Cliff Av CT10 5 C5
West Cliff Dr CT6 11 G2
West Cliff Gdns CT6 11 G2
West Cliff Promenade
  CT11 4 A4
West Cliff Rd,
  Broadstairs CT10 5 B5
West Cliff Rd,
  Ramsgate CT11 4 A3
West Dumpton La
  CT11 25 F1
West Hill Rd CT6 11 H1
West Park Av CT9 20 C4
West Pl*,
  Roseacre Cl CT2 35 E1
West View Cl CT6 11 G4
Westbere La CT2 33 E1
Westbrook Av CT9 18 B4
Westbrook Cotts CT9 19 E3
Westbrook Gdns CT9 18 D3
Westbrook La CT6 11 F3
Westbrook Promenade
  CT9 18 D3
Westbrook Rd CT9 19 E3
Westcliff Rd CT8 18 A4
Westcliff Gdns CT9 18 D3
Westcliff Arcade*,
  Rose Hill CT1 4 C4
Westcliff Rd CT9 18 D3
Westcliff Ter CT11 24 C5
Westerham Cl,
  Canterbury CT2 31 G4
Westerham Cl,
  Margate CT9 21 E4
Western Av,
  Canterbury CT4 37 B5
Western Av,
  Herne Bay CT6 12 A2
Western Esplanade,
  Broadstairs CT10 23 G6
Western Esplanade,
  Herne Bay CT6 11 G1
Western Rd CT9 20 B5
Western Undercliff
  CT11 24 C6
Westfield Rd CT2 30 A1
Westfield Rd,
  Birchington CT7 16 D3
Westgate CT9 18 D5
Westgate Bay Av CT8 17 H2
Westgate Cl CT2 34 C1
Westgate Court Av
  CT2 34 C1
Westgate Gro CT2 6 A2
Westgate Hall Rd CT1 6 B2
Westgate Ter CT5 9 F2
Westlands Rd CT6 11 G3
Westleigh Rd CT8 12 A5
Westmarsh Dr CT9 21 E4
Westmeads Rd CT5 9 F1
Westminster Rd CT1 32 A4
Westonville Av CT9 18 C3
Westover Gdns CT10 23 E1
Westover Rd CT10 23 E1
Westwood Rd CT10 22 B4
Weyburn Dr CT12 24 B1
Wharfedale Rd CT9 19 H3
Whatmer Cl CT2 33 E1
Wheatley Rd,
  Ramsgate CT12 24 D1
Wheatley Rd,
  Whitstable CT5 9 F2
Wheelwrights Way
  CT13 27 B6
Whinfell Av CT11 24 A3
Whitbourne Ct*,
  Essex Rd CT5 9 E4
White Horse La CT1 6 B3
White Post Gdns CT3 27 C2
White Wood Rd CT13 27 B6
Whitefriars Mdw
  CT13 29 E2
Whitefriars Way

CT13 29 E2
Whitehall Bridge Rd
  CT2 35 E1
Whitehall Cl CT2 35 E1
Whitehall Gdns CT2 6 A3
Whitehall Rd,
  Canterbury CT2 6 A3
Whitehall Rd,
  Ramsgate CT12 24 C2
Whiteness Grn CT10 21 E4
Whiteness Rd CT10 21 F4
Whitfield Av CT10 20 D6
Whitgift Ct CT2 34 D1
Whitstable Rd,
  Canterbury CT2 30 B4
Whitstable Rd,
  Canterbury CT2 31 E6
Whitstable Rd,
  CT13
Herne Bay CT6 11 E3
Whytecliffs CT10 23 G6
Wichling Cl CT2 31 G4
Wickham Av CT11 25 G2
Wickham La CT3 38 D1
Wife of Bath Hill CT2 34 C2
Wilbrough Rd CT7 17 E3
Wilderness Hill CT9 3 F3
Wildwood Rd CT2 32 D2
Wilfred Rd CT11 24 D3
Wilkes Rd CT10 23 E5
Wilkie Rd CT7 17 E2
William Av CT9 20 C5
William St CT6 12 C2
Willow Av CT10 22 D4
Willow Cl,
  Canterbury CT2 31 G5
Willow Cl,
  Margate CT9 20 C4
Willow Ct CT10 5 A2
Willow Farm Way
  CT6 13 E4
Willow Rd CT5 7 C1
Willow Tree Cl CT6 13 F2
Willow Way,
  Margate CT9 19 E4
Willow Way,
  Whitstable CT5 10 B5
Willows Ct CT2 30 C4
Willsons Rd CT11 4 A3
Wilmott Pl CT13 27 B5
Wilton Rd CT12 24 B2
Wimborne Pl CT12 24 C2
Wincheap CT1 6 A6
Winchester Gdns
  CT1 35 G4
Windermere Av CT11 24 B4
Windmill Av CT12 22 B5
Windmill Cl,
  Bridge CT4 37 B5
Windmill Cl,
  Canterbury CT1 36 A2
Windmill Ct CT5 9 E5
Windmill Rd,
  Canterbury CT1 36 A2
Windmill Rd,
  Herne Bay CT6 12 D5
Windmill Rd,
  Whitstable CT5 9 E5
Windmill Walk CT12 24 C1
Windsor Av CT9 20 A4
Windsor Cl CT10 23 E3
Windsor Ct*,
  Laleham Walk CT9 20 A5
Windsor Gdns CT6 11 G3
Windsor Rd,
  Canterbury CT1 34 C4
Windsor Rd,
  Ramsgate CT12 26 C4
Wingham Rd CT3 38 D2
Wings Cl CT10 5 D1
Winifred Av CT12 22 C6
Winkle Cl CT6 11 G3
Winstanley Cres
  CT11 25 E2
Winston Cl CT1 36 A3
Winston Ct CT7 17 E2
Winston Gdns CT6 13 F2
Winterstoke Cres
  CT11 25 G3
Winterstoke Undercliff
  CT11 25 G3
Winterstoke Way

CT11
Wolseley Av CT6
Wood Hill CT2
Woodcote CT5
Woodford Av CT12
Woodford Ct CT7
Woodland Av CT7
Woodland Rd CT6
Woodland Way,
  Broadstairs CT10
Woodland Way,
  Canterbury CT2
Woodland Way,
  Sandwich CT13
Woodlawn St CT5
Woodman Av CT5
Woodnesborough La
  CT13
Woodnesborough Rd
  CT13
Woodrow Chase CT9
Woods Ley CT3
Woodside Av CT4
Woodside Rd CT2
Woodvale Av CT5
Woodville CT2
Woodville Cl CT1
Woodville Rd CT12
Woollets Cl CT6
Worcester Gro CT10
Worcester La CT3
Wraik Hill CT5
Wraik Hill CT5
Wrentham Av CT6
Wrotham Av CT10
Wrotham Rd CT10
Wye Gdns CT9
Wyndham Av CT9
Wynn Rd CT5

Yardhurst Gdns CT9
Yarrow Cl CT10
Yew Tree Cl CT10
Yew Tree Gdns,
  Birchington CT7
Yew Tree Gdns,
  Canterbury CT2
Yoakley Sq CT9
York Av CT10
York Cl CT6
York Rd,
  Canterbury CT1
York Rd,
  Herne Bay CT6
York St,
  Broadstairs CT10
York St,
  Ramsgate CT11
York Ter,
  Birchington CT7
York Ter,
  Ramsgate CT11
Ypres Ct CT1

Zealand Rd CT1
Zion Pl CT9

Edition 040 N